The Journal Book

For Teachers in Technical and Professional Programs

Edited by
Susan Gardner and Toby Fulwiler

D1566166

Boynton/Cook Publishers
HEINEMANN
Portsmouth, NH

Boynton/Cook Publishers, Inc.
A subsidiary of Reed Elsevier Inc.
361 Hanover Street
Portsmouth, NH 03801–3912
http://www.heinemann.com

Offices and agents throughout the world

© 1999 by Boynton/Cook Publishers

The author and publisher wish to thank those who have generously given permission to reprint borrowed material:

Portions of "Journals in Medical Education: Experience of a First-Year Class" by Janet Ashbury, M.D.; Barbara Fletcher, M.Ed.; and Rick Birtwhistle, M.D. originally appeared in "Personal journal writing in a communication skills course for first year medical students" by Janet Ashbury, M.D.; Barbara Fletcher, M.Ed.; and Rick Birtwhistle, M.D. In *Medical Education,* Volume 27. Used by permission of the Editor.

"Connecting Classroom and Clinical Experience: Journal Writing in Nursing" by Ann Dobie, Ph.D., and Gail Poirrier, D.N.S. are reproduced with permission of National League for Nursing, from *Writing-to-Learn: Curricula Strategies for Nursing and Other Disciplines,* edited by S. Gardner & T. Fulwiler © 1966, New York: National League for Nursing Press.

Library of Congress Cataloging-in-Publication Data
The journal book for teachers in technical and professional programs / edited by Susan Gardner and Toby Fulwiler.
   p.   cm.
   Includes bibliographical references.
   ISBN 0-86709-453-2
   1. English language—Scientific English—Study and teaching.   2. English language—Business English—Study and teaching.   3. English language—Rhetoric—Study and teaching.   4. Technical writing—Study and teaching (Higher).   5. Business writing—Study and teaching (Higher).   6. Science—Study and teaching (Higher).   7. Diaries—Authorship.
I. Gardner, Susan, 1947–   . II. Fulwiler, Toby, 1942–   .
PE1475.J68   1999
808'.0666—dc21
                                                                98-26723
                                                                CIP

Editor: Lisa Luedeke
Production: Elizabeth Valway
Cover design: Darci Mehall, Aureo Design
Manufacturing: Louise Richardson

Printed in the United States of America on acid-free paper
02 01 00 99 98   DA   1 2 3 4 5

Contents

Foreword

This book is full of happy surprises. It demonstrates how writing in journals and notebooks unleashes the inquisitive and imaginative minds of college students in ways that surprise their teachers, their classmates, and even themselves. Included in these pages are numerous systematic approaches for using student writing to pose and solve problems and to deepen understanding in technical and professional courses.

The Writing-Across-the-Curriculum (WAC) movement in American colleges and universities began in the 1970s and has gained momentum ever since. More institutions than ever before are requiring writing-intensive courses, and more disciplines than ever before are asking their undergraduate majors to develop their written, oral, visual, and electronic communication abilities as an integral component of their professional education.

Before WAC, and before the advent of the information society and the global village, there was an unspoken belief in much of academia that effective writing and speaking were the province of the liberal arts and definitely not the territory of the technical and professional disciplines. Those of us involved in WAC efforts early on assumed that the liberal arts disciplines would be receptive to pedagogical strategies that encouraged active learning on the part of students, interactive teaching on the part of instructors, and increased effectiveness in student-teacher communication about the learning process. One of our first surprises was that such stereotypes were not based in reality. We met literature and philosophy teachers who were completely turned off by the WAC movement's encroachment on what they perceived to be their territory, and we met engineering and nursing instructors, like those represented in this collection, who already used or enthusiastically implemented these additional tools for helping students learn and apply the content of their disciplines.

Suffice it to say that we found teachers in every discipline who found WAC concepts, such as collaborative learning and keeping journals, compatible with their educational goals and values. So while in 1976 we might have assumed that mathematics was a technical discipline that would have very little interest in WAC, by 1990 we were not surprised when The Mathematical Association of America published *Using Writing to Teach Mathematics,* a collection of thirty-one essays edited by Andrew Sterrett. The back cover proudly displays comments from students, such as: "The more I wrote in my journal, the easier it was to communicate in class," and "I try to 'dig' myself out of my confusion by writing down [in my journal] the process I'm supposed to use."

For teachers of a technical or professional course who want students to write in order to generate the knowledge, ability, and enthusiasm necessary for lifelong learning, the first requirement is to be ready for surprise, to expect it, to read and listen for it, and to plan for it. This book—through its numerous extended examples from such disciplines as accounting, computer science, engineering, nursing, and teacher education—shows us how to plan and respond to the surprise that frequently occurs when students and teachers work together through written language to understand disciplinary content—its problems and its possibilities, and its value, usefulness, and connections to other disciplines and other situations. This theme is echoed by Toby Fulwiler in the Afterword to this collection: "The trick here is to present thoughtful and perhaps surprising prompts each week so that the writing never becomes predictable. I want it to be predictable that they will write, but what they write about I want to be surprising." And he concludes by stating: "Since I believe absolutely in the value of writing as a mode of learning, my own best solution is to vary genres, formats, frequency, and media. Emphasize journals one year, letters the next, e-mail the next, and so on." Thus, in classroom settings, the keeping of journals and field notebooks, the exchanging of letters and e-mail messages, as Fulwiler notes, becomes "one place in the academic world where [students] can write and be wrong and not get clobbered for it." Such writing facilitates the mentor-novice relationship rather than the evaluator-test taker relationship, and it creates a language-rich environment in which novices learn from professionals and from each other.

That is what I mean when I write this book is full of happy surprises. Written by teachers from many different disciplines, all of its chapters are applicable to any discipline; they can be adapted from one course to another, from one profession to another. We learn many strategies for building confident learners: traditional and electronic journals, letters, freewrites, focused freewrites, electronic conferences. We use writing that is kept confidential, or shared only with teachers, or only with teammates, or with all class members, and we use writing that generates a written response, or an oral response, or no formal response at all. We see how these teachers assign such writing, why they assign it; we also see the problems they face, the adjustments they make, the successes they have. We read numerous quotes from actual students' writing, and we see students surprising themselves, their teachers, us.

I'll conclude this book's beginning with a "journaling surprise" of my own. I recently attended an interdisciplinary faculty WAC workshop. While talking with a colleague from landscape design, she described how her students do "free sketches" in their journals, a strategy similar to freewrites, in which they quickly, in five to ten minutes, draw a visual of a problem or issue they are working on. Examples she gave were planning a bicycle path between town and campus and designing flower beds for a neighbor's backyard. The idea was to visualize in a very rough way the task, the possible problems, the physical and social context, to get a "feel" for understanding the assignment and for alternative solutions.

With some trepidation, I adapted this technique to my current course in Victorian poetry. At the beginning of class, I asked students to take out their journals and sketch the scene they visualized when they read the poem "Dover Beach" by Matthew Arnold. I told them they could use stick figures or whatever else they wanted to, that this was not an exercise in learning how to draw but rather on how to visually imagine the poem. After about seven minutes, I asked students to share and explain their drawings to each other in small groups, and then I led a discussion of the whole class. The students were as surprised as I was at how this brief exercise opened up the poem for them as individuals and for the class as a whole. We had a lot to talk about and to wonder about. We had discovered together, and we learned from each other in the process, a fresh way to experience and interpret this poem.

I invite you to explore this book; it is a gold mine of surprises.

Art Young, Ph.D., Clemson University
Campbell Chair in Technical Communication

Acknowledgments

We wish to thank several people who have been significant to this book's production: First, Peter Stillman for his continued faith that journals are important and that books like these are a way of reaching audiences who know that and want to learn more. Second, our students in high school, undergraduate, and graduate classes over the years who have taught us much about how journals really work in the classroom. Third, the eleven faculty at Westminster College who took a journal workshop in May, 1994, and sparked the thinking that a book on using journals in technical and professional programs ought to be written. Fourth, the contributors to this collection who wrote and rewrote until we had a text to be proud of and to share with other teachers in technical and professional programs. Fifth, Craig Des Jardins for his computer support in the final throes of editing and sending off the master disks. Finally, Bob Gardner, whose encouragement and support were constant and pushed me (Susan) ahead on this project and Laura Fulwiler, who makes all my (Toby) writing possible.

Introduction

To Use or Not to Use
Journals in a Technical or Professional Program
Susan Gardner, Ph.D.

Writing down your feelings is scary; I don't do this. I write letters to clients. I write to the IRS. I write technical stuff. I feel like I'm talking to myself. That's sick!! I feel sick! I am sick!! I need therapy!! This is making me laugh!! I am sick, definitely sick. This *must* be free writing.

The end. I did it! I'm sorry you have to read this, but it's a START!!
Alan, Professor of Accounting

Eleven professors gathered around the long conference table and turned their eyes my direction. It was my first year in a Writing-Across-the-Curriculum (WAC) position, and these teachers were taking a weeklong workshop on how to use journals effectively in their classes. Quite a disparate group, these teachers were in the fields of nursing, education, accounting, economics, computer science, management information systems, philosophy, and counseling. After using journals in high school and college classes for over fifteen years myself, I felt I had the experience and pedagogy to share with them about integrating journals into their classes.

In preparing for the workshop, I chose Toby Fulwiler's *The Journal Book* (Boynton/Cook 1987), the best and only book describing the use of journals across content areas and levels of education at the time. But knowing that I would have teachers from areas missing in Toby's collection, I began searching periodicals for current uses of journals from each participant's specialty.

Except in the areas of nursing and education, I found next to nothing, or in some cases nothing at all, on the use of journals to help teach in the technical and professional disciplines. Disappointed though I was at not having at least one article for each participant in his or her specific area, I plunged ahead with the workshop.

At the end of the workshop our group realized we had done a lot of good things in our exploration of journals. We read about journals. We wrote journal entries ourselves. We discussed their practical applications. We wrote lists collaboratively to describe our learning of what it is to keep a journal and assign a journal for students. We decided to meet monthly during the next semester and discuss the actual use of journals in our classes. In fact, we even decided to write our own book on the use of journals in these areas often called "technical" or "professional."

For the next year a handful of faculty experimented with journals in a variety of classes. We held monthly meetings to discuss the successes and failures of using journals for the first time in technical and professional classes where students don't always see writing assignments as integral to their learning. Our meetings were lively; faculty were sharing with and learning from each other, taking journals seriously. So, why would faculty in these non-English, non-composition classes want to incorporate journal writing into their classes?

The publication of *The Journal Book for Teachers in Technical and Professional Programs* answers the question. In the past few years professional organizations in areas such as business, nursing, computer science, and engineering have vigorously supported adding more writing in core courses. With the WAC movement in colleges and universities for over twenty-five years now, it is not surprising that disciplines outside the liberal arts have begun incorporating journals into the curriculum. Journals are, after all, a fairly accessible genre of writing to integrate into courses not taught by English or writing teachers.

What Incorporating Journals Can Do

Like their colleagues in the humanities, teachers in technical and professional programs have discovered the power and practicality of using journals. As Bonnie, a nursing professor writing in her required journal for the workshop, noted,

> Surprise! I just realized what I love about learning is the insights and expansion of knowledge I gain. That's what I enjoy about teaching, too. Wow, I want to keep the learning environment fun and accepting for my students. *And,* I'm excited that with writing added to my classes I can share more of their excitement as they experience the "aha's." *And,* I can interact with the quiet students as well as the vocal. Thanks for requiring me to freewrite and think!

Exactly! Bonnie's freewrite points out a number of things journals do for students and teachers. First, journal writing is an additional writing experience for students. Second, journal writing helps students experience the "aha's" of discovering their own thinking and learning, for writing is thinking made concrete. Third, teachers who ask students to write journals gain a window on their students' progress with learning. Finally, teachers can interact with *all* students in a class—not just the more vocal ones.

Diane, a colleague of Bonnie's, expresses the same idea about the importance of finding ways for teachers to interact with students: "With several 'exchanges' throughout the semester of the journal from student to instructor, there is the opportunity for dialogue back and forth." Journals become an avenue for communication and for building rapport between students and instructors when entries are collected regularly and returned frequently enough during the term.

Another nursing professor, Yeou-Lan, struggles with English, finding writing in her native Chinese much easier. Yet, she also senses that, similar to her experience, asking her students to write informally in journals is another way to push them "to understand topics in depth." She has noticed that "through the writing I organize my thoughts and ideas. Before the writing, the thoughts and ideas are 'there' but not really 'there.' . . . I am surprised at how much I know and how much I do not know. This knowing and not knowing surprises and excites me." Having to put words on paper in any form helps her make sense of her reading, her learning, and her thinking about the field of nursing.

Bobbie, a professor of computer science also in the workshop, writes extensively on her pedagogical questions of incorporating journals in an area that changes so rapidly and is so technical. One of the reasons for using journals is to shift some of the responsibility for learning content from her, as teacher, to her students. She comments, "I would like to have my students work through more of the text without my having to guide them through. Granted, sometimes guidance is necessary. One book I used last semester had a lot of scary-looking diagrams (even to me)." Bobbie believes that journal writing on reading assignments could replace quizzes and help students understand the content of the assignment much better.

Another area of concern for her and other teachers in technical programs is that of problem solving. She describes her ideas in another journal entry:

> Another problem that has been bothering me is that many of my students seem either unwilling or unable to attack problems that I think they should be able to solve. Instead of working it out for them, as I did Monday, I could have them write about the problem—identify where the problem occurs, brainstorm solutions, etc. I'm still mad at myself for just telling them how to do it. Where will they learn to solve their own problems?

Writing parts of problems that confuse or block their understanding helps students solve the problems they are assigned to work with.

Another feature of journals is their ability to create active learners in students. A student can be "asleep" while reading an assignment, but no student can be "asleep" and write a journal entry. As Doug Hirt suggests in a later chapter, adding a journal assignment to a large, typically lecture course in engineering promoted active learning among his students. In writing his journal entry for the workshop, John, an economics professor, reflects on passive versus active learning:

> I have long thought that the passive learning model—the ideal of the professor authoritatively feeding students instruction—is wrong. Students, each of us, must ultimately assume responsibility for their learning. Ideally, the teacher is a facilitator, "a guide on the side, versus the sage on the stage." Learning should be an active (activity) process. And writing is one way to accomplish this, one of the most effective ways, for it focuses the mind.

For these teachers in technical and professional programs, then, journals are valuable for the following reasons:

- Journals promote active learning.
- Journals shift the responsibility for learning from teachers to students.
- Journals help students clarify and organize their thinking.
- Journals allow students (and their teachers) to discover what they know and don't know.
- Journals encourage communication between students and teachers.
- Journals help students solve problems or identify their difficulties with solving problems.
- Journals provide informal writing practice.
- Journals give teachers a window on student thinking and learning.

What Worries Teachers About Incorporating Journals into Classes

No doubt the primary fear professors have about assigning a journal in their classes is how to respond to and evaluate them. Should they be graded or shouldn't they be graded? What happens when an assignment is meant to help students open up, take risks, think without fear, and then the journal receives a grade? If it's not graded, then how does it fit in a professional program? The chapters in this book each address the issue of evaluation, providing practical suggestions for how the journal assignment can count for something yet not carry the onus of a grade. Experienced users of journal assignments have wrestled extensively with the problem of evaluation, and those just beginning to incorporate journals will find the suggestions insightful.

Teachers also worry about the increase of paper reading to their already full loads. Will reading journal entries require an even larger time commitment from the instructor? They even wonder if they are up to the task of responding, worrying about their background or lack of background in English or writing. As Alan put it,

> The responding issue is the area that I struggle with because of its importance. I feel right now very uncomfortable responding to someone else's writing. Do I want to sit down and really read what they have written? That is a big time commitment for something that I am going to be uncomfortable doing. This is what English instructors do, not accountants. I can guarantee that I NEVER wanted to be an English person.

How to respond to and how to assess students' journal entries are two large worries teachers in any discipline have when they think about incorporating this type of writing into their classes.

Teachers sometimes wonder if they will cover as much content if they add a journal assignment to their syllabus. Many of the disciplines in the technical and professional areas require "big, fat textbooks" or enormous, detailed syllabi that resemble an entire course pack. Faculty are pushed to ensure that students cover a specific amount of material for their outside boards and national exams. If they opt for more writing assignments, even in the form of a journal, will students get through as much material? Should students actually write some entries in class, or should they share the entries that they have written outside of class? As one teacher told me, her reluctance in using journals is that they take a "large chunk of time" and she wondered if journals are more useful than doing group work to solve problems, a frequent method she currently used.

Another fear, quite related to the issues of time commitment and evaluation, some teachers have is that students won't take assigned journal writing seriously and then they will be stuck with superficial writing because a student just wanted to get the assignment checked off. Stuart, a philosophy teacher who had tried a journal assignment prior to taking the workshop, analyzed the difficulties he had had with the assignment:

> The obvious fear that I had was getting back a personal stream of quasi-consciousness from the students which would be difficult to grade! Or that half the class might skip the assignment entirely or dash off a string of catch phrases before class. Is this overly pessimistic? I am very concerned to give enough structure so that I could grade them. I think I was committed to grading them because I felt that that was the only way to sufficiently motivate my students to do "good" journal writing.

Teachers across disciplines do not appreciate unmotivated, superficial writing by their students, and those in technical and professional areas particularly want to see students grappling with issues, solving problems, applying learning, and so on in their writing. If journals promote clearheadedness and learning of course content, then, they are worthwhile to incorporate. If they are simply a place to ramble, then journal writing won't be the technique of choice for many of these teachers. Many of the chapters in this collection address these fears and provide practical suggestions for setting up journals successfully in a variety of courses.

Finally, technical and professional instructors worry about student reactions to the idea of having a journal assignment. As Bobbie writes in one journal entry, "I know that my students haven't done anything like this in their computer science classes, and I am not sure how to handle their anticipated reactions. Students do get set in their ways."

Sally, a counselor herself, listens carefully to student problems daily. She knows from her own and from student experiences the overload some people go through. In mulling over her busy life in one journal entry for the workshop, Sally candidly wrote: "I find myself avoiding writing journal entries for the workshop. I don't know how much of this aversion is due to past history, where I have avoided it for years, or how much is due to my current stressed situation where I feel like I can't do one more thing!" Students in professional and technical programs are often highly motivated but stretched-to-the-limit type of people. How does an exploratory, risk-taking, reflective writing assignment like a journal fit in with these types of students and their career aspirations? Can the journal be adapted effectively and become a natural extension of the learning in classes in these areas? These are important questions to be answered, and the discussion in the following chapters helps answer some of them.

What to Call Journals in Technical and Professional Courses

Because of the popularity of journal writing in secondary and college English classes during the past fifteen years, college faculty in technical and professional courses may be put off from using them simply because of the term *journal.* Too often people associate *journal* with *diary,* assuming that entries are for gut-wrenching revelations or fuzzy rambling. Associations such as these do not make adding a journal to a professional course appealing.

To solve the problem of association, then, many faculty turn to other terms (and forms) of journal writing. Some alternative terms I've seen used to designate a journal include *learning log, field* or *science notebook,* and so forth. Whatever they are called, journal writing is still journal writing. The writing is still exploratory and often tentative in nature; topics are still student-selected and unfocused although some teachers prefer to provide writing prompts. The physical form of the journal has a broad range. Some journals are done in bound volumes; some are kept in loose-leaf notebooks for ease of taking them out and replacing them. Some are now done electronically through e-mail or word processing. Newer technology seems to be pushing teachers to be both innovative and open in how they put together a journal assignment, and, perhaps, soon students will not be put off by the standard term *journal.*

Keys to Success with a Journal Assignment

Teachers who want to incorporate journal writing into their courses have a great deal of latitude in how that assignment is set up. They can determine what to call it, how it counts in the overall course evaluation, what the journal will physically look like or how it will be done, whether it will be focused by their topic choices or open to student choice, and so forth. Many of the faculty who contributed chapters in this book describe their decisions, uses, and outcomes of journals in their courses. They have experienced the bumps of early assignments and done the refinements to make the journal more successful in subsequent offerings of the class. But, no matter what or how the journal is set up, key ingredients can make the assignment successful or not.

Integrate journals. Don't just tack them on as an additional assignment.
Technical and professional courses are already full—of content, requirements, writing assignments, problems, and so on. If the journal is not an integral part of the course, or of learning the course content in some way, students will resent the assignment. Too often teachers have been to workshops or seen a colleague use journals and decided to use them in courses. They set up the assignment in their syllabus and expect students to produce thoughtful, productive entries with no further support. After all, the journal is an assignment, and students do assignments.

Students will *do* assigned journals, particularly the highly motivated type of students who take technical or professional majors. Teachers who don't "do something" with the journal, don't make it an integral part of the course, however, may be terribly disappointed with the quality of what they receive from students dutifully completing their journal assignment.

To turn this picture around, teachers who set up the journal to accomplish what another form of learning previously did so that the journal can be included in, not put on top of, other requirements often find the power this assignment has for students. Students write entries that genuinely elicit response from their teachers or peers, and that response fuels students' interest in writing further entries.

Use the journals in class. Show they are important to learning.   Students are very astute in observing what is important to their professors. They notice how often a concept is repeated or emphasized in a lecture. They can see the enthusiasm on their teachers' faces when a discussion turns to a favorite topic. They note when teachers seem to take extra time with one of their questions or draft of a paper. All of these instances help students know what is important.

When journals are made important in a class, students can recognize them as important. Journals are important when they are collected and responded to frequently enough so that communication flows between writer and reader. Journals are important when something tangible is done with them. For example, when precious class time is used spontaneously to write journal entries, they seem important. When journals written *outside* of class are used in class to spark discussion, they are obviously valued by the professor. The attention a professor gives to a topic, an activity, an assignment makes each important. Similarly, when a professor assigns a journal at the beginning of a term, never mentions it again as a part of the class, has it turned in only once or twice with long periods of time elapsing before responses are returned, the message to students is very clear: The journal is not important to the professor, not important to the content of the course, and simply an add-on requirement. This kind of journal is neither important nor integral to the functioning of the class.

Conclude with journals. Don't forget them at the end of the term.   The journal assignment can be used productively throughout a term inside or outside of class, but at term's end, it can be a nearly forgotten activity. With formal papers coming due and final examinations taking the stage, the journal is often tossed aside. A final writing activity may prove a better use of students' informal exploration of thinking. Having students reread or review their entries written over the entire term and then write a final entry synthesizing their learning or thinking can be a very rewarding assignment. Such a final activity can help students see their accumulated course knowledge, the changes of attitude they have experienced, and their personal growth as a result of their study. This final entry puts a kind of closure on the journal writing for the course, and students often get a lot of satisfaction out of reflecting on the intellectual and personal journey their journal represents.

So, to Use or Not to Use . . .

The writers in this collection of essays represent a wide variety of professional and technical fields. They are all working professionals. They know the worlds of the medical doctor, the nurse, the engineer, the accountant, the tech writer, the lawyer, and so forth. They are also experienced teachers, and they know the world of teaching from a more career-oriented perspective. All have chosen to use journal assignments as one way to help students in their classes become professionals. These contributors explain their motivation for using journals, describe the actual assignments they gave, and evaluate how effectively the journal worked in their courses. The final two chapters—one on assessing journals and the other on troubleshooting—are especially helpful to those contemplating using a journal for the first time, or those wanting to refine an existing journal assignment. Teachers in technical and professional programs will find a wealth of information in these chapters, whether they are reading about a colleague describing the same field they are in or not. To use or not to use a journal? Read on and then decide.

1

Journals in Medical Education
Experience of a First-Year Class

Janet Ashbury, M.D., Barbara Fletcher, M.Ed.,
and Richard Birtwhistle, M.D.

We talked in the small group about the sessions being more "personal" or "intimate" than perhaps our anatomy groups would be.
I hope that we can use the group sessions not only to learn to communicate with patients and colleagues but also to identify and off-
load some of the stresses we are, or will be, going through. In my
summer job I worked in a hospital in Toronto and on my last day a
clinical clerk (fourth-year medical student) committed suicide, and it
really upset me even though I didn't even know his name. I think
maybe I can see myself getting pretty stressed-out and expect that
I'm going to use this journal as an outlet!

> from the journal of a first-year
> medical student

The transition from a medical student to a caring and responsible physician requires more than a grasp of medical knowledge and technical skills. Medical
students also need to understand and develop effective interpersonal and communication skills. In learning communication skills, students must be encouraged to recognize and ponder their own feelings, assumptions, behaviors, and
expectations and to reflect upon how these issues will affect their ability to
communicate effectively in the medical profession. To facilitate and support
this kind of learning, we have integrated dialogue journal writing into our communication skills course for first-year medical students.

The Course: Learning to Communicate
in a Medical Context

Our course focuses on understanding the key elements of the doctor-patient relationship, the patient's illness experience, and basic interviewing skills. An important goal of the course is to initiate and encourage reflection, self-awareness
and critical thinking. Teachers and students meet together for one three-hour
session each week for ten weeks. In the first hour, during a lecture presentation
for all students, teachers provide background information on topics related to
communication in medicine such as empathy, spirituality, gender, and cross-
cultural issues. Following the lecture is a two-hour session where small groups
of nine or ten students meet to further explore the topic through discussion and
skill-developing activities (role-plays and patient interviews). Two teachers,
(one physician and one allied health professional, a woman and a man) facilitate each small group.

Students memorize little factual or scientific data in this course. Rather, the
course is experiential, and students take away impressions, feelings, and insights that need further exploration. After each session, students describe in
their journals their own thoughts and reactions to the topic and the small-group
session. We ask students to write at least one page in a spontaneous and unedited
style. We encourage students to cover the whole spectrum of their ideas from
personal, introspective thoughts to factual discussions about the topics. Students
are also encouraged to make connections between the course material and their
own experiences and beliefs. For example, a student may be working on the
concept of the doctor-patient relationship. He may write for several paragraphs
trying to clarify and solidify his understanding of this relationship. The student
then may write more personally, describing his own and family experiences as
patients, his expectations and concerns related to the stresses of being a medical student, his suitability to a career in medicine, and his future role as a physician (Ashbury et al. 1993).

Students submit their journals between sessions to their small-group facilitators. Both facilitators write a response to each student's journal entry without corrections for spelling and grammatical errors. Even though a weekly
journal entry is required for the course, teachers do not grade the content of the
journal. Confidentiality is assured, and journals are returned to the students at
the following session.

Though the content of the journal is student-centered and student-initiated,
the teacher is an active and willing participant in the dialogue. In describing dialogue journals, Jana Staton (1987, 56) believes that teachers must be "committed and fully engaged, for it is the teachers' responses which create the motivation and provide the models of thought and reflection, of unpredictability
and honesty which the students need." We as teachers attempt to write nonjudgmental and supportive responses. As with student journal entries, teachers

respond in varied and individual ways. Our responses reflect a wide spectrum of content, length, self-disclosure, and styles. Responses range from more objective, topic-related discussions to descriptions of personal and professional insights and experiences.

Students' Perspectives

From interviews and questionnaires, students tell us that journal writing gives them the opportunity to "string thoughts out," to organize and develop ideas, to reflect on their experience of the course, and to make connections between the course material and their own lives. Many students describe the journal as a safe place where private or controversial topics and opinions can be discussed without fear of being judged.

Students who are often quiet in the small group appreciate the opportunity to share their ideas privately with their facilitator. The students say that the teacher's positive encouragement in the journal gives them the confidence and courage to participate more often during the small-group session.

Most students agree that the responses written by the group leaders make journal writing more worthwhile and meaningful. They enjoy sharing and testing their ideas with someone in the health care field and reading their teacher's experiences and opinions about mutual concerns.

A videotaped interview with a volunteer patient was one of the highlights of the communication skills course. Students anticipated it with feelings ranging from panic to excitement. In their journal after the interview, students discussed their experiences and requested feedback from their teachers. Mark,[1] for example, describes his assessment of his interview.

Today (during the small-group session) we watched our videos that we made a few weeks ago. When I made my video, my impression of the whole experience was that it was out of control. I felt during the interview that the man I was interviewing had total control over the interview and I was unable to direct it at all . . . I realized that I will have to interrupt sometimes, and that the interruption must be done as politely as possible. Also, hand gestures and body movements can be good cues to use to let the patient know that you would like to interject something . . . All in all, I feel that I learned a lot from watching and analyzing all of the videos, even though my video was not very good.

The facilitator responds personally, validating and supporting the interview as a useful learning experience: "Especially at your stage of your education, what makes a video good is how much you can learn from it. I know how painful it can be to watch yourself perform, but as you have found, this can be an extremely effective and efficient learning process. Remember that it is the process that is to be judged, not you as a person."

Another student described his experience interviewing an elderly woman with an illustration.

Figure 1–1

The main drawback of journals for students is having to produce journal entries by a specified deadline when they can't think of anything to write. These students say that they would rather be assigned a specific question or problem. Other students prefer to express themselves verbally in the small group. Some students find writing in the journal too time-consuming.

Some students are also reluctant to write about themselves. They relate their hesitation to many issues, including concerns about trust, confidentiality, and the teacher's power in possessing such personal information about a student. These concerns have also been identified by Grauerholz and Copenhaver (1994). Students acknowledge that this hesitation and anxiety usually decreases within a few weeks as they come to know, through the dialogue, that they can trust their facilitators not to judge or criticize their ideas.

Teachers' Perspectives

All of the facilitators agree that journal writing is an essential and valuable component of this course, providing a "longitudinal thread," connecting one session to the next. When we first started this course seven years ago, we anticipated that the teachers' involvement in journal writing would be minimal, taking only a few minutes of our time to read the students' journals and to jot down a few brief remarks. However, as teachers we found ourselves drawn into the process as students shared personal life experiences and insights. Few of us were satisfied with a superficial and distant role. We became active participants in the journal dialogue.

The weekly journal provides a "window," allowing teachers to observe, to some degree, each student's thoughts, perceptions, and depth of interpretation of the same session. Quiet students have a voice and share their experience of the course in their journal. We see students' ideas evolve and the individual insights that students gain.

We also learn from the students' feedback in the journal about the course, small-group dynamics, and ourselves as group leaders. Getting suggestions and evaluative feedback from our students about our teaching encourages us to be reflective learners ourselves.

Responding involves many considerations and challenges. This kind of ongoing, personal involvement with journal writing takes considerable time and reflective thought. On average, teachers spend two to five hours a week responding to nine or ten journals. Some students write lengthy discussions and stories, sometimes up to ten pages. In these situations, teachers have to set their own limits of time and length of response.

Teachers say that in order to write meaningful responses, they must withdraw physically and emotionally to reflect upon their students' thoughts. Obviously, then, responding can't be done between patients during a busy clinic or while watching television at home. Many teachers have commented on the difficulty of scheduling specific, quiet journal time into an already full clinical, research, and teaching workload.

We noticed how self-reflective journal entries tend to be more interesting and engaging to read than detailed accounts of the information discussed in the session. We encourage students who appear to restate the major points of a didactic presentation to personalize what they have learned. For those who cannot or do not include more personal comments, we respect and acknowledge that the journal belongs to the student. It is the student who decides what to write and what not to write in the journal.

We found responding difficult when the entries were oppositional or antagonistic. We try to understand the student's perspective and then present our point of view in a constructive way. We also try to find a balance between encouraging a student's views and challenging him or her to consider a different opinion. In the journal, the risk of misunderstanding by both the student and the teacher always exists. Thus, we try to stress that the journal is a place for discussion and clarification of each other's ideas, especially if comments are perceived as judgmental or critical. This emphasis on communication reinforces the dialogue component of the journal.

All teachers question at times the quality and usefulness of their responses for the students. Sometimes, the facilitators of the same group meet to talk about their students' journal entries and responses. These discussions help develop rapport between them as facilitators and responders.

Issues Beyond the Journal

The use of dialogue journal writing in the communication skills course has highlighted some teaching issues that have repercussions beyond the journal itself. These areas of interest and concern lend themselves to further exploration.

The Teacher's Role

Ideally, in our responses, teachers model an "empathetic provocateur" (Mezirow and Associates 1990, 366), a caring and nonjudgmental listener who supports but also challenges the students to further explore their own attitudes and beliefs. This model seems appropriate for teaching within a caring profession like medicine (Fletcher 1993, 77). We encourage and support self-reflection by sharing our own experiences where it is appropriate and relevant to the student's journal entry. We drop our objective role as an expert to become a person to our students, "not a faceless embodiment of a curricular requirement nor a sterile tube through which knowledge is passed from one generation to the next" (Rogers 1983, 122).

As facilitators, we attempt to imagine and understand our students' ideas and experiences so that we can respond with useful feedback. We often draw upon insights learned through our own personal and professional experiences in order to reflect back to the students our impressions of their situation. In this way, students may get some helpful direction in seeing, shaping, and developing their identity as people and physicians.

The following example illustrates this process of "reflecting back" (Burley 1997). In his journal entry, Allen describes the connection between his family experiences and his pre-medical school assumptions about the role of the physician. He goes on to tell how the course and the small-group experience have changed this viewpoint and helped him to reach a new understanding of the doctor's role.

> When I was a teenager my parents divorced and I was thrust into the role of "man of the house" for my mom and my two sisters with whom I lived. The role of "man of the house" meant I made up the budget, I filled out the taxes,

I dealt with the important household matters, and I received a lot of positive reinforcement to assume this role. My mom and my sisters were looking for a strong head of the household, and I assumed that role. I think this was the beginning of the time that I started to suppress all emotions. Without this communication skills group, I would probably approach medicine with the same attitude, i.e.: the doctor must be without emotions, the great stoic and calming force in the situation. But this message you have been saying—the doctor is human, and the patients want the doctor to be human—is a message that hasn't been lost on me. I have gained a new outlook. . . .

In his response, the facilitator "reflects back" to the student, describing his own thoughts about the student's experience as a young man:

Boy, what a time for your parents to divorce. At sixteen, we are in the thick of one of the most important developmental crises in our lives. We are trying to separate and develop a sense of ourselves as individuals. Right in the middle of this for you, you were thrust into a situation where you weren't allowed to do this, but had to become (whether you were ready or not) an adult overnight. Not only that, but it sounds as though there wasn't much time or place for your own "grief" over the loss of your family as you had come to know it. It's not surprising that you began to suppress your emotions . . . there was no place for them. You have it in you. . . . It is possible and allowed to be a man and a doctor and a husband and father who shows himself and his vulnerabilities as well as his strengths and direction. . . .

At times teachers respond empathically as they recognize themselves in their student's experiences. The following excerpt from a journal illustrates such a response. In her journal entry, Jenna openly describes her perception of her personality and relates this to journal writing, her small group, and becoming a doctor.

You can't know how much I like the idea of journals. I've always been able to express myself more openly on paper. This seems like a strange paradox to me. It is courses like these that give me the most stress (because I rate myself as a poor communicator), yet here I am, given the opportunity to tell my feelings in the way I find least difficult . . . I'm a quiet person by nature. I don't expect to change and I don't really want to change, at least not drastically. I still prefer to have a few close friends rather than hoards of acquaintances. There I go—I have a bad habit of justifying my shyness. You said that doctors with different characters learn to do what works for them, in order to establish rapport with patients. I guess what I'm basically getting at is, I hope that it is possible to find something that'll work for me without me having to become a person that I'm not.

Today, my anxieties were alleviated somewhat. I found out that the fears that I have in abundance are probably present in everyone at least to some degree. People who looked so cool, confident, and collected to me, admitted that they were nervous or uncomfortable in some situations.

The facilitator, while being empathetic and supportive, shares similar feelings.

> Thanks so much for your honest and insightful comments and feelings about yourself and the group. I can sense your fear and concern about your "quiet" nature and how that will affect your learning and future role as a physician. To be honest, I have often felt some of those insecurities and fears and I continue to battle with them now. I have often wished that I was more outgoing, could make a group laugh, could shed my introverted personality, and feel less intimidated by extroverted outgoing people . . . More and more, I have become less critical of myself and I have realized that quiet does not mean uninteresting, boring, or useless. . . . In the doctor-patient relationship, qualities like genuineness, honesty, and respect are far more important than being an extrovert . . . I wanted to reassure you that what you wrote in your journal this week was what we want to see—something personal about the session and personal connections to what was discussed . . .

The following week, Jenna responded to her facilitator's comments, and the dialogue continued:

> First of all, thanks so much for your encouraging answers. Lately my roommate has been repeatedly reminding me in subtle ways that I won't be a good doctor unless I become less quiet and antisocial. It's been difficult to keep my chin up. I am very hard on myself and the last thing I need is another person emphasizing my weak points. I do a very good job of that on my own. Your responses really gave me that extra strength that I need right now . . .

The Teacher's Responsibility

By encouraging self-awareness and reflection, the dialogue journal has opened the door for students to disclose personal stresses, illnesses, and conflicts. Some students described strong personal memories and beliefs that arose from controversial and sensitive topics such as death, sexuality, racism, and violence. Students shared with their facilitators personal and health problems such as eating disorders, depression, anxiety, and suicidal thoughts. The journal offered a private place for the expression of these issues. We believe that this is one of the most positive aspects of journal writing in our course.

However, we realize that we must consider where our responsibility lies when students disclose personal struggles and ask for advice and help in their journals. All teachers agree that the journal is not a place for therapy, though at times we tread a fine line between giving support and providing counselling. We must be careful not to confuse our role. In many cases, we have assisted students in seeking professional help, and teachers have used the journal to privately follow up on the student's progress with his or her problem.

Education around issues of physician stress and vulnerabilities needs to start in medical school. Physicians are known to have a high incidence of marital problems, depression, suicidal risk, and alcohol and drug abuse (Baird et al. 1995, 260). Personal unresolved memories and conflicts can later interfere with a student's ability to provide adequate patient care and blind them to the needs of their patients (Bethune and Duke 1994, 2069). It is also beneficial for teachers to be aware early on of potential difficulties that their students might be experiencing. Through the journal, we give our students the important message that expressing these concerns and worries is acceptable and healthy and that they should seek help if necessary.

In the quote already cited at the head of the chapter, Sally describes a tragic experience and relates it to journal writing, the small-group sessions, and being a medical student.

> We talked in the small group about the sessions being more "personal" or "intimate" than perhaps our anatomy groups would be. I hope that we can use the group sessions not only to learn to communicate with patients and colleagues but also to identify and off-load some of the stresses we are, or will be, going through. In my summer job I worked in a hospital in Toronto and on my last day a clinical clerk (fourth-year medical student) committed suicide, and it really upset me even though I didn't even know his name. I think maybe I can see myself getting pretty stressed-out and expect that I'm going to use this journal as an outlet!

Here the facilitator supports Sally's request and goes on to share some of her own beliefs.

> I totally agree that the small group will be a place to vent anxieties, stresses, etc. Last year we did it when we realized the need. This year we have longer sessions so that we will have more time for that. The need for medical students to "care for themselves" is crucial. It seems however that as they become socialized into the profession they become further and further distanced from themselves and their needs, thus the incredibly tragic consequence you described. I believe that physicians/nurses/therapists etc. must first care for themselves so that they can adequately care for others. Therefore, let it be resolved that you and I will ensure that this will be an integral part of this course.

Teacher Recruiting

Teacher recruitment is an important consideration in this course. Because of the active participation of the teacher in dialogue journal writing, it is important that teachers be chosen carefully, taking into consideration their teaching styles, personalities, and commitment to the importance of journal writing and the goals of the course. Like most teaching strategies, we realize that dialogue journal writing is not for everyone.

Since new and experienced teachers have expressed a need for more direction in approaching their multifaceted role in this course, workshops have been presented periodically. Teacher retention is a potential problem. The time commitment combined with the energy drain in responding have caused teachers to "step out" and take a break from teaching this course every two or three years.

Teacher concerns about time and responding have forced course planners to examine more closely the rationale for using journals and responses. Would journal writing be useful if teachers did not write responses? At this point, most if not all teachers agree that the responses are an essential component of journal writing in our course and that the benefits for students and teachers of this written dialogue outweigh the drawbacks.

Final Thoughts on Using Dialogue Journals

Our experience has shown that journal writing individualizes and personalizes the teaching and learning of communication skills. Dialogue journal writing plays a significant role in diminishing barriers between the students and ourselves as teachers, and rapport is enhanced. The essential elements of this rapport parallel many characteristics of the doctor-patient relationship: confidentiality, trust, respect, and genuine interest. Within this caring environment we encourage our students to explore and share their thoughts, feelings, and questions about the course in relation to their past and present experiences and their future roles as physicians. As Longhurst (1989, 72) noted, "The doctor must acquire the broadest possible awareness of his own feelings, needs, and conflicts to bring the greatest good to the healing act." It is our hope, that given this chance, they will be better prepared to deal competently and compassionately with the complex needs of their patients.

Acknowledgments

We are indebted to the first-year medical students and teachers at Queen's University in Kingston, Ontario, Canada, who gave their personal consent to allow us to quote from the journals. We thank the students and teachers of this course (past and present), who generously gave of their time, sharing their ideas in discussions and questionnaires. Also we wish to thank Doug Babington, Joe Burley, and Ted Ashbury for their most helpful interest and input with this chapter.

Notes

1. In an attempt to make the use of student samples similar to those in other chapters, the editors have inserted fictional names for many of the quotes in this chapter.

Works Cited

Ashbury, J. E., B. M. Fletcher and R. V. Birtwhistle. 1993. "Personal Journal Writing in a Communication Skills Course for First-year Medical Students." *Medical Education* 27: 196–204.

Baird, N., J. S. Fish, M. Dworkind and Y. Steinert. 1995. "Physician, Heal Thyself: Developing a Hospital-based Physician Well-being Committee." *Canadian Family Physician* 41: 259–63.

Bethune, C. H. and P. S. Duke. 1994. "Listening to Their Stories: Disclosures and the Dilemmas." *Canadian Family Physician* 40: 2068–69.

Burley, H. J. 1997. "Dialogue Journal Writing and the Process of Reflecting Back." Personal correspondence.

Fletcher, B. M. 1993. *Journal Writing as a Reflective Tool in Medical Education.* Master's project, Faculty of Education, Queen's University, Kingston, Ontario.

Grauerholz, E. and S. Copenhaver. 1994. "When the Personal Becomes Problematic: The Ethics of Using Experiential Teaching Methods." *Teaching Sociology* 22: 319–27.

Longhurst, M. F. 1989. "Physician Self-awareness: The Neglected Insight." In *Communicating with Medical Patients,* ed. M. Stewart and D. Roter, 64–72. Newbury Park, CA: Sage Publications.

Mezirow, J. and Associates. 1990. *Fostering Critical Reflection in Adulthood: A Guide to Transformative and Emancipatory Learning.* San Francisco, CA: Jossey-Bass Inc.

Rogers, C. 1983. *Freedom to Learn for the 80's.* New York: Macmillan.

Staton, J. 1987. "The Power of Responding in Dialogue Journals." In *The Journal Book,* ed. T. Fulwiler, 47–63. Portsmouth, NH: Boynton/Cook Publishers.

2

Connecting Classroom and Clinical Experience
Journal Writing in Nursing
Ann Dobie, Ph.D., and Gail Poirrier, D.N.S.

Today was a shock to my system. Right when I feel confident in my abilities to get things done on time BAM!!! I get hit with the rush of surgery transit. While reading the consent form and before we even began to fill out the pre-op check list, it's hello transport probably two minutes after the doctor left the room. . . . That evening I ran into my patient's wife at Albertson's [grocery] while shopping. She said that the surgery ended at 6:30 and that her husband would probably be paralyzed from the waist down. I offered my sympathy and prayers. She seemed very grateful and really happy that he was alive.

from a student journal

Anyone who has been in a hospital or doctor's office recently knows that the American health-care system is undergoing dramatic reforms. While patients are becoming aware of changes in how they are treated, the caregivers already recognize their new roles and responsibilities. Today's nurse knows that she is not what she used to be. In fact, these days *she* is very likely to be a *he*.

Regardless of gender, today's nurses find themselves with a wide variety of opportunities and duties they have not traditionally had. They are managing clinics, working to meet the needs of diverse populations, and using computerized information systems to better plan and provide care. They are concerned with prevention, education, and care management (in addition to treatment), and they are relying more and more on outcomes data and evidence. Entrusted with more authority and responsibility for decision making than ever before, nurses are increasingly called upon to analyze (as well as collect) data; to communicate effectively with colleagues, patients, and their families; and to think critically about the health care of patients in their charge.

To respond effectively to the rapidly changing roles of nurses, educators have over the past decade carried out their own quiet revolution. They have traded in the lecture-only mode of information giving for computer searches, the teacher-as-authority model for collaborative projects, and outdated curricula for courses that address contemporary concerns. Many of these changes have encouraged teachers to introduce writing into nursing courses, not simply in the traditional form of research papers that demonstrate a student's understanding of professional format and documentation, but as writing-to-learn strategies designed to enhance a student's recall of data, comprehension of concepts, and application of theory. As a result, today's nursing students are expected to be more than good note takers, memorizers, and scantron markers. As Susan McLeod (1987, 20) points out, they are expected to be active learners who build their own knowledge structures through such critical-thinking processes as analysis and synthesis, problem solving, and evaluation.

Why Use Journals?

One of the chief means of introducing complex thinking and learning processes into the nursing classroom has been the journal. Although it is hardly a newcomer to such classes, over the past decade journal writing has assumed a larger (and still growing) role in the professional development of health care givers.

Journals are effective learning tools for nursing students in large part because they invite personal reflection, a deliberate and conscious activity that permits the individual to contemplate behavior and events and responses to them. As such, reflection is of special importance to those who are entering a profession filled with difficult emotional experiences and ethical quandaries. Nursing is not simply a technical field; it has a humanistic, caring dimension that requires practitioners to cope with more than the physical concerns of their patients. To do so means exploring sensitive feelings, buried attitudes, and undefined values. It requires developing the capacity to deal with others' emotional complexities as well as one's own.

For example, a short journal entry, like the one that follows, allows a student to resolve personal uneasiness with clinical experiences by the written release of emotions and feelings. One anxious student, Maria, commented, ". . . I couldn't help but worry about this baby the whole time we were at the hospital and he has been on my mind since then. I wonder if he improved or got worse. This experience makes me wonder how I will react if this or any other baby that I care for dies. It really scares me" (quoted in Reynolds 1996, 86).

In the following entry another student went beyond her own feelings to explore those of her patient. Her comments show her to have been deeply attentive to the state of mind of the person she was dealing with. Brooke wrote:

> She is so lonely. She was overjoyed to have a student nurse care for her this week. She shared many feelings with me. She alternated between funny, joyful replies to my questions to suddenly becoming fearful. I asked her what her greatest fear was and she replied that she did not want to suffer. I talked to her at length about the availability of medications to help make her more comfortable, and although at first she seemed doubtful, she later did call her nurse and ask for one of her PRN medications. . . . (quoted in Reynolds 1996, 87–88)

Reflection can also have an ethical dimension. For instance, emotional discomfort with what Libby observed in a clinical situation led her to question the rightness of the behavior of the caregivers. The disapproval she intuitively felt became a defined ethical stance in writing. She said:

> I think this particular patient I cared for was getting very poor care from the nursing staff. She sat in her own feces for 2–3 hours because her nurse didn't come when she first called, and the client did not want to bother her again. Even in her routine daily care, the nursing aides would not wash her hair the day before I took care of her, they just said no! I would be so frustrated in her position, everyone else deciding what is best for her, irregardless of her feelings (quoted in Reynolds 1996, 86).

Whether an entry serves to resolve uncomfortable personal feelings, understand a patient better, or define professional values, journals promote the caring side of nursing that focuses on human beings and their health. In that process, journal writing may also lead to changes in current behavior by facilitating different future actions.

Because such personal investigation leaves the nursing student exposed and vulnerable to challenge, the nonthreatening nature of the journal makes it a particularly appropriate medium of analysis. Unlike the essay test question or the pop quiz or formal exam, the journal provides relative safety for students to question, probe, and hypothesize. Freed from the need to find a "right" answer, they are able to observe themselves and contemplate what they find. In the course of questioning personal perspectives about issues and practices that make them uncomfortable, nursing students often address topics they might never have mentioned to an instructor or peer in a classroom directed by more traditional strategies. Journals become a means for private communication between teacher and student. As one student commented at the end of a course:

> The journals provided me an outlet for thoughts on the clinical experience that might not have been brought to my conscious arena had I not taken the time for the entry. . . . Even though they added to my work load, they allowed me to voice my feelings and experience about important aspects of my clinical day.

It also allowed the instructor to become aware of what was happening with me that day in clinical. I enjoyed the freedom of being able to choose important aspects of the day to write about rather than being told specifically what to write about (quoted in Reynolds 1996, 90).

Self-reflection in the context of professional concerns leads inevitably to discovery—about oneself and about one's profession. When such events occur, the journal becomes a record of personal growth and development. As the clinical journal is a written record that reflects attitudes, feelings, and learning throughout a nursing course, it is the instrument through which new understanding can be traced, tested, and understood.

Celina, a student who had a particularly poignant experience with an elderly patient, spoke of her own personal and professional growth in this way:

> This week was different for me in home health. I spent time with a patient who was suffering and who would soon face death. It was hard for me not to cry. I am so thankful for the things I have after looking at this patient's living conditions. As a future nurse, I want to become actively involved in environmental and policy-making issues to better help the elderly.

Journals in nursing can produce equally effective discoveries when they are turned outward, away from the purely personal toward finding connections between reading, writing, thinking, and learning. They can provide opportunities for students to synthesize theory and practice, apply relevant research and literature to clinical situations, and raise questions and concerns for further study. As Reynolds points out, the clinical journal "provides students a guided opportunity to 'think aloud' on paper, reflecting on their own perceptions or analysis of the situations they encounter in the clinical area" (1996, 84).

One student, Steven, worked through to some conclusions about a patient as he wrote about her:

> If you really *listen* to this client, and talk to her, not at her, you will find that she is confused. She is not sleeping well, she is taking tranquilizers, and so she does forget and needs reminding and reinforcement. I don't know too much about the availability of support groups, but this client and her husband really need to talk to someone who has been through this situation before, to tell them what to expect, to show them that life can go on normally; to basically give them hope. [The client had suffered a major stroke.] I had a long talk with her son, he just did not want to believe she would never walk again. We talked about things that his mother would be able to do, we discussed wheelchair ramps. . . . We both felt that his mother would do better in the hospital if she had the same staff members assigned to her as frequently as possible. . . . she needed more continuity and familiarity. . . . (quoted in Reynolds 1996, 87)

It can be argued that journals are more appropriate for some courses than for others, that some classes lend themselves to commentary more readily than others. While that may be so, it is also true that regardless of the concerns of a course, journals can help nursing students to engage in personal reflection about their ethical values and professional growth, enhance communication with their patients and their instructors, and provide a way to deal with problems that involve both theory and practice. In short, they help students to acquire and construct knowledge, gain maturity, and grow professionally.

Where Does the Teacher Enter This Picture?

Nursing instructors play a new role when they introduce journals to their classrooms. They renounce the lecture podium and encourage student involvement. On occasion they even join in the discussion through their responses in dialogue journals. More generally, they move from being classroom autocrats to being classroom managers who arrange and schedule the writing experiences. Finally, they eschew their judges' robes to become coaches and guides.

Take, for example, the question of how to maximize the effectiveness with which journals are used. Because nursing students will make best use of them if they understand their purpose from the outset, the instructor's task is to make clear the expectations for each journal assignment and its relation to course unit objectives and conceptual content. The teacher will explain, for instance, how the time and energy required will enhance students' understanding of course content, develop their critical-thinking skills, or improve their problem-solving abilities.

When an instructor chooses to assign topics for journal entries, they will be as varied as the issues covered in a course. The only requirements are that they should provide for active learning, and students should never be able to interpret them as a punitive measure. They may be concerned with trends, research, or politics. They may be used to raise ethical concerns or designed to promote professional growth and development. For example, they may ask questions about a patient's right to die, or they may ask for a description of meaningful interactions or experiences that students may have had with other health-care providers. Some assignments may involve an extension of class notes, or they may directly address unit objectives. In lecture/discussion courses that require understanding relationships between concepts, the assigned topic may require students to examine connections — such as those that exist between the concept of curing and actual application of nursing knowledge in clinical settings. Other suggestions for writing may be more personal, asking students to state their learning objectives for the week or to describe significant activities that occurred during the course of the clinical day. They may call for students to record their personal reactions (their thoughts and feelings) to particular challenges of the clinical experience. The common thread in all such assignments is that they pose questions about or ask for comments about nursing that have no exact or absolute answers.

What Form Should the Entry Take?

Because many instructors use journals as an out-of-class activity, or one that takes a minimal amount of class time, students are often left to choose the form of their entry. Specific strategies available for use include most writing-to-learn techniques, since the purpose is to push the writer to incorporate new knowledge, develop a more complex understanding of the conceptual topic, and address different audiences.

Nursing students and instructors alike can easily adopt or adapt the following techniques for developing an entry.

Brainstorming

A noncritical, unrestrained list of suggestions and ideas. Usually done as a group, the process can be carried out by an individual.

Assignment Example: (a) Write negative statements for five minutes about a powerfully emotional topic—e.g., death and dying—in an effort to explore the characteristics of a painful subject and your own attitudes toward it. (b) Generate a list of cost-effective nursing health-promotion measures to assist persons with chronic illness.

Sample from a Student Journal:

I hate taking care of patients with AIDS! I feel helpless—it's like staring death in the face. Death is ugly in these cases. AIDS strips people of life too early and confuses family and friends in a hurtful way. The financial problems and social isolation caused by AIDS is overwhelming for most patients and families. I don't think I could deal with this.

Buddy Exchanges

Dialogues in the form of letters that can be exchanged between classmates to help them clarify course content. Such exchanges often begin with a statement of an opinion, a problem, a general misunderstanding, or confusion regarding course material.

Assignment Example: Write a critique of another student's Interpersonal Relationship paper (written report of a real patient/student communication experience). You should make your analysis from both a personal and an academic perspective.

Sample from a Student Journal:

This IPR demonstrates lack of therapeutic communication skills. You have a tendency to give a lot of false reassurance like saying "it'll only take a second" or "it'll be all right" when you can't generate either one of those. Put yourself in the patient's place.

Dialectics

Notes from readings recorded on the left side of a page and comments or questions about the material read on the right side of a page.

Assignment Example: To explore your own professional ethics, respond to an assigned reading (or to notes from a lecture) by writing on the right side of the page how this material affects you personally.

Sample from a Student Journal:

This lecture on caring for a paraplegic came to life for me today in clinical practice. I learned how lucky I am. I take for granted the "able" body I was born with. When I want a drink, I get it myself. When I need the bathroom, I go to the bathroom and don't depend on a bag for that purpose. I complain about my weight and features when in fact I have no problems compared to these patients.

Exit Slip

A brief entry written at the end of class summarizing what has been covered or explaining some important point about the day's topic.

Assignment Example: After listening to a lecture related to culture, health, and illness, use the last ten minutes of classroom time to write a short paragraph stating why it is important for you, as a provider of health care to individuals, families, and groups from cultures other than your own, to understand your own beliefs about health and illness.

Sample from a Student Journal:

The study of cultural diversity in health and illness is important for nurses because our understanding of *other* cultural beliefs allows us to properly treat our clients and value *their* health beliefs and practices. It is important for the nurse to be aware and accepting of cultural diversity to ensure compliance and understanding of prescribed regimen by the patient. The study of cultural diversity in health and illness is important for nurses so that they may deliver the best and most appropriate care to the consumer.

Focused Writing

A short, intense, nonstop, timed writing on a single topic that can be introduced spontaneously at any point in a class.

Assignment Example: Write negative "self-talk" related to skills testing and performing the same interventions for the first time in a clinical setting.

Sample from a Student Journal:

What if I forget the sequence of the procedure? Why can't we just give the enema without all this fuss—it's a simple procedure. I know I'm going to fail because I'll forget to instruct the patient how to breathe during the enema. There are so many things to do all at one time—let water in slowly, squeeze the clamp, talk to patient. I don't know if I'll manage this skill especially if I get a picky instructor—I'll have to remember to breathe slow and deep too!

Freewriting

A short, intense, nonstop, timed writing that is not bound to a single topic.

Assignment Example: Write for five minutes, beginning by talking about your "best" clinical learning experiences and why they were important to you.

Sample from a Student Journal:

One great learning experience was when I put in the Foley catheter. I was very nervous because performing a procedure on a rubber dummy in LRC and a live breathing human are definitely two different things. I'm glad I was able to do this procedure because now I feel like I know what to do and what to expect from a "real" patient during this common procedure.

Lecture and Readings Summaries

A recapitulation of major points and explanations.

Assignment Example: List the major points of wound care as discussed in your textbook, giving supporting examples of each procedural step.

Openers

A quick entry at the beginning of the class period that helps students bring to mind content from the preceding class or from the assignment for the day.

Assignment Example: Write your goals for the day, specifying both theoretical and clinical learning goals.

Sample from a Student Journal:

At the end of this week's clinical and classroom experiences, I will be able to:

1. Define loss, grief, and death.
2. Describe loss as crisis.
3. Describe Kubler-Ross' stages of grieving.
4. Discuss assessment of the grieving patient.
5. Discuss assisting patients to "die with dignity."

Problem-Solution Explorations

A clear definition of a problem (or a cluster of problems) followed by a listing of possible means of solving them, ending with an evaluation of the solutions' efficacy.

Assignment Example: Develop a list of positive communication techniques to use when caring for terminally ill patients, angry patients, and family members.

Sample from a Student Journal:

Conflict management involves assertive communication skills. When I communicate with angry patients, I speak calmly, rationally, and use factual statements. Active listening is important—it tells the angry party that you respect their feelings. Look at the person, not just the conflict. If you stay focused and use assertive techniques, you can handle conflict.

Unsent Letters

A form of role-playing that requires students to write letters to someone outside the class or as a person involved in the material under discussion.

Assignment Example: As a graduating senior, write a letter to practicing nurses, other health-care providers, or nursing instructors that discusses the effects of positive and negative models of assertive behavior on the improvement of student learning outcomes in clinical settings.

Sample from a Student Journal:

One thing that bothered me was the lack of concern or apathy that my charge nurse seemed to have about the change in my client's condition. When the charge nurse is organized, everything seems to run smoothly and thus the learning process is great! I can accept and expect reprimand. But please show me a caring and understanding attitude. You were also a student once but now you're a nurse—so act like a professional role model.

How Does a Teacher Respond?

Once students have produced a sizable amount of writing, an instructor ultimately has to *do* something with it. Some kind of response is mandatory, though most teachers agree that grades are rarely the answer. In fact, giving grades to journals can be especially problematic in nursing studies because it can effectively block the reflective skill that should be developed by journal writing. Students are quick to realize that writing in an open, honest manner places them in an extremely vulnerable position, making them fearful that they will alienate or offend their instructor. As Paterson points out, "When the risk of expressing one's ideas freely is associated with the possibility of failing a clinical course, students are unlikely to use journal writing as an opportunity to explore and analyze their thinking about the profession" (1995, 216). Instead, students are more likely to respond favorably to an open classroom environment, one that allows self-expression and sensory stimulation. As one student put the case: "I found them especially helpful when I was allowed to write on what I considered meaningful to me. I did not find them as useful when the instructor dictated what was to be written, as I did not always feel the freedom then to express my true feelings" (quoted in Reynolds 1996, 90).

Another problem with awarding grades to nursing journals is that criteria for evaluation are difficult to formulate. For one thing, typical academic concerns, such as grammar and spelling, are not relevant issues here, since clinical journals are not formal, scholarly papers but an ongoing dialogue between student and faculty. For another, journal entries will vary in length and quality; they may not be about the same topics or take the same forms. They are personal documents that invite personal response.

Several alternatives to grading are available. The instructor may choose to make one or two overall comments about an entry, encouraging the student to raise additional questions for further exploration or analyzing and evaluating the student's observations and perceptions in relation to theory and research. If a more judgmental response is called for, the instructor can award bonus points, or indicate the quality of an entry by a satisfactory/unsatisfactory marking or a check-plus-minus system. In general, however, students find journals to be most rewarding when they are ungraded, nonpunitive, and open to constructive criticism of specific content or conceptual understanding.

While recognizing the negative effects of grading journals, instructors who are disappointed by the quality of those they read sometimes feel the need to report their dissatisfaction. When the writing fails to reflect the anticipated critical thinking or authentic self-reflection, some kind of evaluation can be helpful to the student. On those occasions when a grade seems appropriate, part of the final course grade can be based on the student's having made a genuine effort to fulfill the journal requirement. The simple fact of having carried out the assigned task with diligence can be counted as having fulfilled what was required, thereby giving it weight in the course requirements.

The Last Word

In the classrooms of nursing instructors who expect a high degree of student involvement, journals have proven to be of exceptional value in promoting student questioning of clinical experiences, their reflection on personal attitudes and values, and their professional development as caring individuals. Journal writing also provides students with the opportunity to improve the quality of their writing over the course of a semester. Instructors who give students this opportunity must be willing to give up some degree of control, allowing them the right to make choices and express personal feelings and opinions. Instructors must be willing to add the role of guide and correspondent to their more traditional ones of authority and judge. Although they may retain their lecture stance as a means of disseminating information, they may also discover through the use of journals a powerful means of relating the data and concepts of the lecture to the personal experiences of their students. When that happens, a rich dialogue of critical thinking between student and self, student and teacher enriches the learning experience.

Works Cited

McLeod, S. 1987. "Defining Writing Across the Curriculum." *WPA: Writing Program Administration* 11 (1–2): 19–24.

Paterson, B. L. 1995. "Developing and Maintaining Reflection in Clinical Journals." *Nurse Education Today* 15: 211–220.

Reynolds, S. W. 1996. "Journal Writing in Nursing." In *Effective Writing-To-Learn Strategies for Nursing Curricula,* ed. G. Poirrier, 81–93. New York: National League for Nursing Press.

3

Developing a Professional Identity with Journal Reading and Writing

The Advanced Composition Course for Nursing, Social Work, and Pharmacy Students

Sandra J. Balkema, Ph.D.

This article caught my eye for two reasons. One reason was that I had not heard of Meniere's disease and wanted to know what it was. Another reason was that this article was written by a nurse. I think sometimes we as nurses forget that we can become ill, too. I am guilty of this type of thinking. I guess I think of myself as being shielded by a great wall that protects me from any real life threatening or chronic problem. It was interesting to hear a nurse's feelings from the perspective of the patient role. Nurses are said to make the worst patients because we carefully and critically watch our care.

Diane, a BSN student

Journal Reading and Journal Writing

A few years ago, a group of my pharmacy students who were going through the spring internship and job-search process were panicking as they tried to prepare themselves for countless interviews. Their worries centered, I discovered, on the fact that they didn't feel comfortable expressing their professional plans and interests. They could cite the facts and figures they'd been learning in their science courses, but they didn't know how to talk about their professional identity and future.

This discovery led me to incorporate journal writing into my classes, primarily my upper-division advanced composition courses that are part of the Writing-Across-the-Curriculum (WAC) project. With many others on college and university campuses across the country, I've been involved in an active, vital WAC project stressing the importance of developing the writing skills of graduates in all fields, from professions such as social work in which recording objective as well as subjective observations is crucial, to nursing and allied health professions in which concise, accurate objective details are critical to patient and client care.[1]

In many of these colleges and universities, WAC takes the shape of writing-intensive courses designed by content specialists and taught by these same people. On other campuses, this opportunity presents many traditional writing teachers with the opportunity to move beyond writing classes with heterogenous populations into more homogeneous classes with students from the same academic programs.

Three of the classes I teach within our WAC program are for specific disciplines: Social Work, Pharmacy, and Nursing. These classes are homogeneous, and the assignments all center around rhetorical situations central to that field. Social Work students write case reports, practice subjective- and objective-reporting styles, and write project proposals; Pharmacy and Nursing students write patient-information materials, protocols, and research reports. All three of the courses were developed following accreditation requirements and with the assistance and cooperation of the program faculty.

While all of these students need to develop their mechanical writing skills—and each of their accreditation boards or program faculty stress this, all of the boards also stress the need for the students to have strong critical-thinking skills and awareness of professional issues and concerns. The formal writing assignments develop the students' awareness of the rhetorical aspects of situation, audience, format, and style. Reading professional journal articles and writing informal reactions to these articles heighten their awareness of their own views and opinions and help them develop an awareness of their professional selves.

The Assignment

The journal-writing component is quite structured, for a journal assignment. Students write journal entries of two types: reaction entries and bibliographic entries. I evaluate both on content and amount of effort (what I call mental involvement) and not on mechanical correctness. They submit their journal entries in even-numbered weeks throughout the semester for comments but receive a grade only at the end of the semester.

The reaction entries link directly to the formal writing assignment in progress: They may ask for the student's reaction to a chapter in the textbook or prompt the student to practice a principle we've been discussing in class. For example, when the nursing students are drafting their patient-information materials, their journal assignment has them critique an existing piece, do a readability test on it, and test a patient's comprehension.

The bibliographic entries are the more interesting of the two types, for they prompt critical thinking in a less structured approach that can elicit enlightening, often exciting comments from the students. The requirements for the bibliographic entries are basic: Students read one article from a different professional journal (an entirely different journal, not a different issue of the same journal) for each entry. Students choose the journals and the articles based on personal interest. This spreads the students into a variety of different professional journals and may even lead some of them to redefine their definition of their field and shape their specific interests within their field. For the nursing and pharmacy students, I suggest a mix of journals representing trade journals, research journals, and those representing specialty settings (such as operating-room nursing or retail pharmacy).

Once they've read the article, they write a brief summary (1–2 paragraphs) of the article including the bibliographic data for the article. They follow the summary with at least a page of their views, opinions, ideas, and reactions. The mental involvement component, on which I base their grade, is often the difference between the student writing a general comment ("This concept is one we've discussed in our genetics class last semester") to a direct, concrete experience ("We studied this in genetics, and I never understood how it worked until I read this article!"). I tell them that I want them to look for implications, to tell me what the issue means to them as professionals.

What the Students Gain

As with all forms of journal writing, what the students gain far exceeds my modest assignment expectations. On a cognitive level, they become familiar with professional journals in their field, decide if each journal is or will be valuable to their future, discover if each journal is a purchase they can afford or a career necessity they can't afford to ignore, and realize that professionals like themselves write and publish articles of use and interest to them. In one of the reaction journal entries, described above, students write a brief description of each of the journals they used for the bibliographic entries. They include the audience, purpose, and focus of the journal; they also cite the subscription cost and summarize the manuscript submission requirements.

On a more subtle level, they gain a great deal more. By writing their reaction to, analysis of, and ideas about the articles, these students are writing to learn—about themselves. They gain confidence in their knowledge and training, shape their opinions, define their professional goals, and create a professional identity for themselves. While many of these discoveries overlap and merge in their writing, their journals speak for the importance and value of each discovery.

Writing to Learn . . . What They Know

As the students read the professional literature, they often realize that what they're learning in the classroom has a direct connection to what they'll do every day on the job. This recognition develops a confidence in their professional training. In many ways, they're discovering that they know something of value. Jamie, a nursing student, for example, chose an article on conscious sedation because of a new job responsibility:

> I chose this article for a variety of reasons. Currently, I am working on becoming credentialed to administer I.V. conscious sedation. . . . If those who are administering I.V. conscious sedation are not kept up to date on current medications and consistently monitored as to the competency of their skills, the improvement of care will decline rapidly. . . . This article was a wonderful resource for me. . . . I feel much more informed and comfortable with my new role and responsibility. The information regarding the legal criteria necessary to administer conscious sedation is invaluable. The policy and procedure manual given to me at work does not discuss this criteria. Before I accept this new responsibility I need to make sure the criteria listed in the article are in place to protect me legally.

Recognizing that one's training and professional knowledge has worth and is recognized as valuable is an important step in developing a professional identity. The flip side of the students' discovery of what they know is their recognizing the limits of their education and the need for continuing education. If they run into an article that they do not understand or do not like, I encourage them to analyze their reaction, to try to figure out why they had difficulty. This, too, is a way of defining their professional limits. When Julie wrote early in the semester of her broadening awareness of the possibilities available in her profession, she was taking a step which, by the end of the semester, led her to decide to research master's degree programs:

> The process of determining policies fascinates me. I never realized how much input you can have if you participate in your professional organizations. I used to think that everything was cut and dried concerning what you can and can not do. . . . I never imagined that my scope of practice would include more than what I was taught in nursing school.

Sometimes the students' journal entries provide me with information about how clearly (or if) my messages about "good" writing are getting through. Sue and Kellie, both BSN students, in writing of their frustration, discovered the importance of audience awareness, reinforcing the rhetorical principle stressed in every one of their class assignments. As Sue described it, she commented

> This article was incredibly confusing and not one bit helpful to me. In other words, I disliked it very much. If I had to tell someone about the AMA and how to get information, I would tell them to stay the heck away from this article! . . . Let's put it this way: I think the article has important information to express, but I don't think that I was the correct audience for this article.

Kellie echoed the same kind of frustration:

> I read this article three times the first night and read it two more times the night I wrote this entry. After a great deal of contemplation and help from my fiancé I began to understand the general idea behind the article. Initially, I felt my difficulty in comprehending the material was because I am not a member of the target audience. The article was geared toward management and has little to do with the practice of nursing. However, the article was specifically geared toward the problems of an observation unit and left out a large number of its audience members.

Roger, too, stumbled on the importance of clear organization and efficient placement of visuals in his journal entry:

> I thought that this might be an interesting paper to read; instead I found that it was difficult to follow and understand. I guess this paper was hard for me to follow because much of the article was showing a cost model and algorithm of cost function that used a table containing over 30 different symbols of characteristics for formulas that were used in the paper. Most of the paper was formulas. I was constantly looking up what the definition of a symbol was and this was very distracting to my reading.

Writing to Learn . . . What They Believe

As they discover the extent and limits of their factual knowledge, they also begin to shape their opinions. When their journal writing prompts them to discover what they believe, they take their professional identity beyond the restrictions of an entry-level follower into a potential for leadership. This ability to express their opinions is often the aspect of the journal writing the students find the most exciting. They spend most of their academic lives taking in information; the time and place to let out their ideas and opinions are often lacking. However, at times their personal opinions will have a direct bearing on the ability to perform their job. Thus, identifying their beliefs can be essential to their professional lives.

In writing their views on controversial topics, Colleen and Kevin faced the fact that they might be asked to resolve a conflict between their personal beliefs and their professional responsibilities.

> Colleen: This article deals with the debate of assisted suicide. . . . This topic is now affecting us in Michigan as Dr. Jack Kevorkian has attended a 32nd death. I agree with the points of agreement on end-of-life care. I don't agree

with assisted suicide and my reasons are mostly due to my religious and moral beliefs. . . . If there is a time that assisted suicide becomes legalized there are going to be a lot of health care professionals making difficult decisions. I hope that day never comes.

Kevin: This article is about genetic testing to predict if a person is predisposed to getting cancer later in life. This article is written by a freelance pharmacy and medical writer. She did a good job of stating both sides to this story in a neutral, unbiased manner. I think that genetic testing will be an important part of medicine in the years to come, but it likely will be controversial for some time to come, too. . . . I think that a person who has a family history of cancer at an early age would benefit from this type of testing. . . . The problem these patients could face, though, is discrimination from health and life insurance carriers if they were to find out about possible debilitating and expensive health problems.

Angie, a pharmacy student from Puerto Rico, often brought her international perspective to the issues she wrestled with. She also frequently addressed the differences between her personal beliefs and experiences, and the party line most of her American pharmacy colleagues believed.

The author is informing non-U.S. readers of the movement in this country to make health care more accessible to everyone, not just to those who can afford it. To me this article is like a progress report since many of the readers live in countries where a universal health system has been in place for decades. While I agree that ideally everybody should have equal access to medical treatment, I am leery of the government defining the issues, directing the resources that are privately generated and the establishment of yet another bloated, unresponsive bureaucracy.

Several of the students identified problems faced by their supervisors and the issues they might face if they were in similar positions. Sarah and Diane both wrote about their concerns and expressed, with the confidence of a Monday-morning quarterback, the decisions they would make.

Sarah: [This] article is targeted mainly at health care executives that might still be in the dark on how to access the Internet and harness its technology to serve their organizations. . . . Computers and the Internet can become double-edged swords, however. Obviously, technology by itself will not make the decisions for the managers. Before they can make good use of the information available to them, health care administrators must first clearly identify the mission of their organization and understand well the environment in which they are operating.

Diane: Recently I worked with someone who stated that he had trouble assessing dark-skinned people. I was so upset that he could complete a nursing program that did not bother to teach him this skill. I wrote a letter to the president of M_ Hospital and described the above incident. I asked that he educate his employees with some sort of cultural diversity classes. . . . This article made me remember my letter to the president but also I am reminded that this is a problem all over.

Writing to Learn . . . What They Want

For many of the traditional students who have made career decisions while still teenagers, as they prepare to graduate, they face questions and doubts about their professional goals. Nontraditional students, too—though supported by more life experiences, as well as more successes and failures—are making decisions about specialties, work environments, and lifestyles. Reading professional journal articles representing various specialties and the issues faced by practicing professionals can help them as they make these decisions.

Angie's plans for her future directed her reading for the journal entries:

The Journal of Social and Administrative Pharmacy is clearly targeted to pharmacists in the position to affect policies and procedures in their organization (a.k.a., as the "big cheeses"). These administrators must be aware that their decisions cannot be made in a vacuum and have serious consequences on living, breathing persons for good or bad. . . . I will definitely be interested in subscribing to this journal after graduating from the Pharm.D. program since I anticipate some day to be in a position to actively advocate for financially sound policies that are also sensitive to the plight of the growing segments of our population unable to equally access quality pharmacy services and products: the elderly, poor, the homeless, and under-served minorities.

Colleen and Kristi both wrote of their awareness of the changing workforce and the need for versatility and goals.

Colleen: This article focuses on how downsizing and decentralizing, role shifting, work redesign, and health care networks affect nursing. . . . All of the suggestions given in this article were realistic. . . . I was surprised to read in the article that some staff nurses make $60,000+ and should consider that in these times they won't find many jobs that will match that salary (the 60,000+ is what I was surprised about!!) Nursing is changing and will continue to change due to hospital restructuring and health care reform. . . . We all need to think about the future and have an idea of where we are going and where we want to be going.

Kristi: This article gives me a sense of optimism, yet it scares me to think that if companies are competing for employees, then graduates are going to be competing just as hard for those available positions. This means that I will need to analyze just what it is that I am after well before graduation.

As these students look at the demands of a changing world and the need for lifelong learning, they also look to the authors of these articles for answers and direction. The expertise Catherine and Kim see represented in the professional journals is of the "real world" and gives them an important contact to the broader needs of their profession.

> Catherine: The author wrote this article to inform the readers of what being a home health nurse is about. She states at the end of the article that this type of nursing makes her feel great and wouldn't choose another. The article was interesting and did sound like something I would like to try. . . . In every job there is going to be something that you don't really care for, and I can't believe that home care nursing is perfect. In this article I would have also liked to hear about a day that she felt that she couldn't help all of her patients and what she does about those feelings.

> Kim: I found this article to be a good source of information concerning my field of study. . . . Maybe if I keep myself posted on what is going on, when I graduate I will have a better education and finely tuned skills. . . . I feel that this article has shed some light on the path that I am going to be taking in school. I have elective courses that I need to take and after reading this article and several others like this, I think that I will focus in on studying more about the sales end of my marketing degree.

Writing to Learn . . . What They Share

As with any academic assignment, this journal-writing assignment is going to be more useful for some students than others. "Good" entries are more likely to come from those with a prior commitment to their chosen profession and a desire to be an active part of that profession. Thus, for students who are ready to take up the challenge of leaving the safety and security of college life and move into the realm of professionalism, it is a perfect opportunity for them to shape their professional identity with little threat or risk. But it can also prod those students who assume their college degree is the ticket to a perfect job in a perfect life; it can get them to face some realities- –good and bad. It also gives them the chance to see their profession through fresh, almost naive eyes, and see the possibilities waiting for them. Over the semester, Kellie, Diane, and Jamie used their journal entries to express their astonishment and, sometimes, bewilderment, at the vagaries and weaknesses of their profession.

> Kellie: Academically the nursing profession has been confusing for a long time. I am a member of this profession and still find it challenging to keep up with the various credentials available.

> Diane: I'm amazed that many institutions are not subscribing to the different publications available. I would want my employees to have resources avail-

able that could help to educate them on current trends. . . . we have a lot of outdated journals and we need current journals!

Jamie: My dream is for the medical and nursing professions to come together and offer the public all they have to offer. No more competing or feelings of superiority or inferiority. We are different not better or worse. Together we have a lot to offer.

Evaluating the Journals

At the end of the semester, when they've written their last journal entry and their last formal assignment, I ask them to evaluate the journal-writing assignment by identifying the journal they found most valuable and what they found most beneficial about the assignment. I ask them to identify the criteria they use (or plan to use) when subscribing to a journal: the cost, an affiliation with a professional organization, a focus on research, a focus on practice, a mixture of research and practice, or what? Did they like reading the articles because they enjoyed (a) reading about issues currently of importance in their field, (b) reviewing various professional journals to "see what's out there," or (c) writing their reactions on topics of professional concern to get a chance to find out what they really think about them? These brief fill-in-the-blank comments are usually mixed; each student looks a little differently at the journals and the assignment.

On the course evaluation, however, where the students evaluate each assignment and weigh its value to their careers, the reaction is always a strong positive. Few students will deny the benefit (and even enjoyment) they get from a low-pressure, high-return requirement that allows them to contradict their teachers or employers, spout off about their favorite pet peeves, stand on their soap boxes, or think aloud, and then be rewarded for it. Jamie, one of the more observant nursing students, for example, evaluated the assignment this way:

Throughout this semester, I have read articles from various types of journals and magazines associated with nursing. The different types included trade, hospital, and research. I became aware of journals and magazines I had never read or heard of. I found some to be quite cumbersome and others to be a gold mine. All in all, I find it exciting to have so many professional reading options. I feel I am a member of a "true" profession.

As for me, I too, learn about the professional journals in their fields, the issues of importance, and watch the process these young professionals follow as they express their opinions and discover the value of their place within their professions. I continue to enjoy the opportunity their journal writing gives me to learn while reading over their shoulders.

Notes

1. There are many articles that discuss the necessity for good communication skills in professions across the board and the value of directed writing assignments as a key component of professional development activities. See the chapter references and especially De-Simone (1994); Hobson and Schafermeyer (1994); Leach and Sandall (1995).

References

Ashworth, T. and D. E. Vogler. 1992. "Writing-to-Learn in Freshman Nursing." *Journal of Studies in Technical Careers* 14 (1): 1–10.

Ault, D. E. and J. F. Michlitsch. 1994. "Writing Across the Business Curriculum: An Alternative Means of Developing and Assessing Written Communication Skills." *Journal of Technical Writing and Communication* 24 (4): 435–47.

Bidwell, L. D. M. 1995. "Helping Students Develop a Sociological Imagination through Innovative Writing." *Teaching Sociology* 23 (4): 401–6.

Brennan, M. J. 1995. "Essay Writing in Nursing: Alerting Students and Teachers to the Educational Benefits." *Nurse Education Today* 15 (5): 351–56.

De-Simone, B. B. 1994. "Reinforcing Communication Skills While Registered Nurses Simultaneously Learn Course Content: A Response to Learning Needs." *Journal of Professional Nursing* 10 (3): 164–76.

Gibbons, D. C. 1995. "Unfit for Human Consumption: The Problem of Flawed Writing in Criminal Justice and What to Do About It." *Crime and Delinquency* 41 (2): 246–66.

Goza, B. K. and A. D. Lau. 1992. "Hiring Practices for Human Resources Professionals: Implications for Counseling and Curriculum Development." *Journal of Employment Counseling* 29 (4): 172–79.

Hobson, E. H. and K. W. Schafermeyer. 1994. "Writing and Critical Thinking: Writing-to-Learn in Large Classes." *American Journal of Pharmaceutical Education* 58 (4): 423–27.

Holiday-Goodman, M. et al. 1994. "Development of a Teaching Module on Written and Verbal Communication Skills." *American Journal of Pharmaceutical Education* 58 (3): 257–62.

Leach, J. A. and D. L. Sandall. 1995. "Required Business Skills for Training Professionals." *Journal of Industrial Teacher Education* 32 (4): 74–86.

Painter, C. M. 1985. "A Survey of Communications Skills Needed On-The-Job by Technical Students." *Journal of Studies in Technical Careers* 7 (3): 153–60.

Shulman, G. M. 1993. "Using the Journal Assignment to Create Empowered Learners: An Application of Writing Across the Curriculum." *Journal on Excellence in College Teaching* 4 (1): 89–104.

Stewart, C. and L. Chance. 1995. "Making Connections: Journal Writing and the Professional Teaching Standards." *Mathematics Teacher* 88 (2): 92–95.

Wade, C. 1995. "Using Writing to Develop and Assess Critical Thinking." *Teaching of Psychology* 22 (1): 24–28.

Watkins-Goffman, L. and G. J. Dunston. 1994. "Writing Across the Curriculum in a Data Processing Class: An Ethnographic Investigation." *Research and Teaching in Developmental Education* 11 (1): 31–35.

4

Encouraging Active Learning
Adding a Journal to Engineering Lecture Courses
Douglas E. Hirt, Ph.D.

> I could follow the example you worked until you chose the velocity scale. I don't understand why you chose the maximum velocity. . . . Ah, yes, but the plot of v vs. x would be a little different, right? I think I answered my own question.
>
> from a student journal

One of the most difficult tasks a faculty member faces in the classroom is getting students to become active in the learning process. Several methods can be used to promote active learning, such as asking questions and waiting (sometimes at length) for a response, dividing the class into groups and asking them to address a particular issue, having students work problems on the board, or even having them do the lecturing. But it is often difficult to implement some of these techniques, particularly for classes with a large number of students or for technical courses that are typically lecture-driven and that involve numerous equations and definitions. Additionally, these methods consume class time—a precious commodity when a teacher feels pressured to cover the topical content outlined in the course catalog.

In an attempt to involve students in the learning process, I have used some of the techniques described above in several engineering courses that I have taught. Dividing the students into groups to solve problems, typically referred to as collaborative learning, is a successful method and well worth the effort (Felder 1995), but the other techniques use class time unproductively. Therefore, I have used journal writing to encourage the students to become more active in the learning process without sacrificing class time. These journals are used for informal writing, giving the students the opportunity to express their thoughts and questions about course-related issues and about issues outside the scope of the course.

Journal writing is certainly not a new concept. It has been used frequently in liberal arts courses, and it has also been used for many years in science and engineering courses, although the body of literature describing journal writing in engineering is more limited.[1] Selfe and Arbabi (1983) used journal writing in a civil engineering lecture course and required students to write at least one page per week about the course, including documenting progress on design projects. The pages were submitted for review three times during the ten-week quarter. I used a similar approach except that the journal writing was not required, but those who elected to write in a journal turned in multiple pages each week.

Schulz and Ludlow (1993) used student journals in a different way in a graduate chemical engineering course. The students were required to write journal entries (comments and questions) about assigned reading before attending each class. Each submission was evaluated on a scale of 1 to 5. In the work described in this chapter, however, the journal entries were made after class, and the submitted pages were not graded. Obviously there are many ways to integrate informal writing into a lecture course such as Fulwiler (1987) and Marwine (1989) describe. The purpose of this chapter is to provide the framework that I have used to incorporate journal writing into chemical engineering courses and to use examples of student writing to illustrate the benefits of informal writing.

Practical Considerations for Assigning a Journal

The majority of the courses in which I have experimented with journal writing have been on the junior and senior levels with enrollments from thirty to sixty students. The students were not required to submit journal pages—they did so on a voluntary basis. The instructions were provided to the students at the beginning of the semester, and the weekly assignment was always the same. At the end of each week, the students could submit a journal page, from each previous class period, describing the most important thing(s) that they learned from those lectures. The objective was to encourage the students to go back into their class notes, review the material, extract the important information, and transfer their thoughts about the subject matter onto paper. The students were then free to write on anything else.

Journal pages from the previous classes were handed in each Friday (or Thursday for a Tuesday-Thursday class) and *checked off*. I told the students that the pages would *not* be graded for grammar, punctuation, or political correctness. In addition, I stressed that the information that I read in each student's journal pages would be held strictly confidential. The incentive for submitting all journal pages was two bonus points at the end of the semester, making it possible for a student to have a final course grade of 102. It should be emphasized that the students were *not* required to submit journal pages, but, for juniors and seniors, the two bonus points were incentive enough so that over 90 percent of the students participated in this activity through the entire semester. Recently, I taught a course to engineering freshmen on problem-solving skills and offered them the same incentive for turning in journal pages. Only 10 percent of the freshmen participated in the journal writing, which may say something about the freshmen perception of the value of writing or bonus points or both.

Journal pages were collected at the end of each week and read over the weekend. Oftentimes students asked questions about lecture material or homework problems. It took approximately one hour per fifteen students to read all of the pages and give written feedback to questions. Feedback ranged from short answers to lengthy derivations to words of wisdom. I debated whether to edit the writing by making spelling and grammar corrections, but I made the decision that it would be too time consuming and that it was not necessary for this type of informal writing (although in a few glaring instances, I did point out to students that they needed to improve their spelling).

Examples of Journal Entries

As mentioned earlier, the goal of journal writing is to encourage students to be more active in the learning process. For this to be successful, the students must make an attempt to truly understand the material and ask questions if something is not clear. The value of the journal writing is illustrated below using examples of student writing.

In a journal entry, Ted commented:

> Liquid-liquid extraction is a process in which a liquid solvent is used to extract a solute from a liquid mixture. Is liquid-liquid extraction the same thing as "solvent extraction"? I do not remember what the object of the separation was (what was to be separated), but I know that kerosene was used as a solvent. The separation was accomplished in tall columns with a series of plates inside. The walls of the columns were transparent, so the plates inside were visible. These columns were about 15 to 20 feet tall.

Here Ted took what he was learning in one course and related it to something that he had seen before. An objective of journal writing is to get the students to realize that there are connections between various topics in engineering (e.g., between heat transfer and thermodynamics). In my experience making connections does not occur with great frequency (although I note an exception in a later example), probably because it is easier to view one subject at a time without considering the bigger picture. It is gratifying to see students relating lecture material to their everyday experiences and to their industrial work experiences.

In one of her entries, Susan asked, "Could you explain why the second homework problem only has pressure from gravitational forces and the first problem has to account for both pressures (I'm not sure I understand the difference)." The question Susan posed is an example of the most valuable aspect of journal writing. Many times students are apprehensive about asking questions in class or visiting the instructor in person. Journal writing provides a nonthreatening environment for asking questions and receiving feedback. It is also valuable for me as the instructor because when I find common questions raised in journal pages, I can clarify those issues in following class periods. Journal writing thereby provides me with weekly feedback from students.

All instructors would like to see an entry such as the one Sharon posed, which opens this chapter. She begins by setting out her problem and then comes up with the solution on her own, a good example of how writing can be used for learning: "I could follow the example you worked until you chose the velocity scale. I don't understand why you chose the maximum velocity. . . . Ah, yes, but the plot of v *vs.* x would be a little different, right? I think I answered my own question." Unfortunately, this type of entry is not encountered often enough, but occasionally journals demonstrate what a professor hopes they will.

For example, the following two entries by Christine, made several days apart, illustrate first her insight and then her creativity:

I have finally begun to notice an interesting trend this year among my classes. Finally, all the little bits and pieces of information and skills we have been taught in the past 2.5 years are coming together. For example, we are using Laplace transforms from math class to solve problems in Process Dynamics. We can use Numerical Methods to solve problems in all other classes. Also, in many instances, PChem and Thermo go hand-in-hand. I find this trend very encouraging and helpful—courses reinforcing each other.

I have discovered that I am a Bingham tanner. Yes, once our design project was turned in, I suddenly found a wee little bit of free time. So I used it to lie in the sun for 1.5 hours one day last week to rid myself of my ghastly color. Even though it was a very sunny day, with a temperature in the 70s (°F), and even though I (unwisely) wore no sunscreen, you would not have been able to tell (on the following day) that I had ever gone outside. I figure that I must reach some minimum value of sun exposure before I tan.

George asked a very good question in the following example, and then added a bit of humor to his inquisitiveness: "Can diffusion ever occur 'up' a concentration gradient?"

"Space for professor to enlighten student."

I also encourage students to write about other things, particularly items related to engineering (newspaper or magazine articles, TV shows, seminars, discussions with friends, and so on), and about personal experiences if they so desire. Most of the students stuck to course-related issues, but many students wrote about unrelated topics, including significant others, interviewing, politics, other classes, tests, lack of sleep, and (usually toward the end of the semester) their philosophy of life. I did not try to discourage writing on these subjects because I wanted to give the students the freedom to express their thoughts and to solicit my opinion or feedback on various topics.

When students write freely, anything can happen. For example, a particularly interesting example came from Mary's journal:

> Forgive me Professor for I have sinned. It has been a long time since my last honest journal entry and I have been, although harmless, a wicked student as viewed through the eyes of the true and scholarly. I have slept on the couch rather that finishing P. chem lab reports (of course this was after a night of cramming organic). I have basked in warm sunlight while 'studying' for a test (not yours, I assure you), and I failed to submit the last unit operations homework for correction. To further add to this insult, the reason for my shortcoming is not a valid excuse (which explains my hesitance in requesting that I be permitted a deadline extension), but rather that I was irresponsible and went out to play before my work was finished. Yes, I could probably have arranged to present solutions to the problems, but the work would not have been mine own, thus doing neither of us any good. I would not have spent the required time and effort to understand the material and the grader's analysis of 'my' work would have been faulty since it would not have reflected 'my' understanding of the subject. From this I hope you see my lack of self-discipline and youthful misdirection was not intended as an insult to you or your class, but rather a vow to myself to finish the assignment before the problem session so that I could learn from my own mistakes. I was successful in completing the assignment, with some tutoring from caring friends, finding my many mistakes through your explanations, and correcting my errors. If I were a bold individual and ventured to ignore your promise to not bestow credit on tardy homework, I would say my work scored 6 or 7 out of 10. But I, not being that brash nor bold, would not mention this, but rather thank the Professor for the xerox plot (which cleared up many questions) and humbly hope that honesty will soften my zero recorded in the ominous grade book when an esteemed Professor, such as yourself, reviews the record of my semester's work. By the way, I had a blast at the concert.

This kind of journal entry becomes playful in its use of archaic, semiconfessional language. My written response continued the banter:

> I, with not a plethora of trepidation, concur with your bold and yet humble statements. An old wise man once said, "Those who basketh in the sunlight

turn into lobster and all knowledge leaketh out." I, too, would like to enjoy the fruits of my leisure time, but my only opportunity these days seems to be around 10 p.m. in these hallowed halls . . . I have duly noted the zero in the grade book and I ponder, is this a true reflection of the knowledge of this aspiring chemical engineer? Does she not understand the concepts of gas absorption, which to me are trivial compared to the strenuous work required to get a tan? How can I convey to her, my esteemed colleague, that the meaning of existence may be found in gas absorption? I cannot fathom, nay, it is incomprehensible to me how this learned person, with all of her knowledge and unbounded enthusiasm, can succumb to these extracurricular pressures. Yet now after grading the latest challenge, there is great joy in Mudville, for the aspiring chemical engineer/writer has done well . . . Maybe, just maybe. . . .

Assessment and Suggestions

In the Spring semester 1993, Clemson University's Pearce Center for Professional Communication administered a survey to my junior-level chemical engineering class to obtain student feedback to journal writing. Students were overwhelmingly positive about the experience, although a few said that it took too much time and a few had not written any journal pages. These juniors (and seniors in a subsequent class) said that journal writing:

- helped identify key concepts
- helped them retain information more easily
- provided an opportunity to get clarification from the professor
- was a place to speculate about the practical applications of the course theory
- gave them a chance to know the professor more personally

The last item was particularly important to me. Journal writing not only gave the students a chance to know me more personally, but it gave me the opportunity to know them as well. This interaction through journal writing and response seemed to create a more relaxed atmosphere in class, and students seemed less afraid to ask questions. In essence, journal writing indirectly led to an active-learning environment in the classroom.

Initially, I was met with some resistance when I proposed the idea of journal writing. The students were skeptical ("honestly, I thought the idea of a journal in my engineering class was stupid at first, but the journal proved useful") and, frankly, I did not know what to expect. After several semesters, however, the process has evolved so that it is a valuable tool for the students and for me.

I do have some suggestions for teachers wanting to try integrating journals in their engineering courses. I think the following tips help make journal writing a more positive experience, both in terms of student learning and faculty time.

Stick to the concepts.   In the beginning, too many students strayed from the original intent of the journals and wrote about everything except the course. The instructor must emphasize that journal pages will not count unless they focus on at least one major concept from each lecture.

Help students be more than transcribers.   The other extreme occurs when students simply transcribe class notes onto journal pages. The professor should emphasize that students must summarize the lecture by selecting, for example, one to three key points and making some thoughtful comments or asking some questions.

Be moderate in numbers of journal entries to read.   If a teacher is faced with large classes or severe time constraints, have students summarize important points from each week of lectures on one page. They still identify key points, but students tend to write less when they are limited to one page. As an alternative, collect journal pages every few weeks and selectively read some of them as Selfe and Arbabi (1983) suggest. The disadvantage to periodic or selective reading is that a teacher does not receive weekly feedback.

Provide an incentive for students to write.   I offer an incentive for students participating in journal writing. I found it amazing how many students, especially upperclassmen, will write when offered two bonus points for submitting journal pages throughout the semester. As one student commented, ". . . The two bonus points for my average were highly motivating."

Summary

A key question for me as a professor is whether journal writing has an impact on learning. Diab and Kloser (1996) conducted a study in which they evaluated the performance of students in a science course taken by nonmajors. Three sections of students did not use journal writing and formed the control group while three sections of students did use journal writing. The academic abilities, course content, and exams were all comparable between the two groups, so any difference in performance was deemed attributable to the effect of journal writing. Diab and Kloser performed statistical analyses on the two groups and reported that the students doing the journal writing scored significantly higher on course grades than the control group. This study, which was performed over several years, reinforces the hypothesis that informal writing can enhance student learning.

As the instructor, I found journal writing by my students to be beneficial. It gave me the opportunity to answer their questions directly with written feedback and also allowed me to identify common questions that could then be addressed during subsequent class periods. The journal also provided a forum for students to express their opinions on a variety of topics. As an outside assignment, journal writing takes no class time, and it is a valuable means of communication between students and the instructor. More importantly, it motivates students to review lecture material and to write about it on a regular basis, a practice we should all follow to document our thoughts and ideas. I close with a telling student comment made after the semester was completed: "Although at times it was a pain, it allowed me to get things out. Strange, but I have continued writing journal pages. . . ."

Acknowledgments

I would like to thank Professors Art Young and Chris Benson from the Pearce Center for Professional Communication at Clemson for their helpful advice and interaction. This chapter was based on an article entitled "Student Journals: Are They Beneficial in Lecture Courses?" published in *Chemical Engineering Education* (vol. 29, p. 62–64, 1995).

Notes

1. For examples of general uses of journals in science and engineering, see Beall (1991) and (1994); Borasi and Rose (1989); and Halsor and Heaman (1991). For more specific information on journal writing and engineering, see Selfe and Arbabi (1983) and Schulz and Ludlow (1993).

Works Cited

Beall, H. 1991. "In-Class Writing in General Chemistry," *Journal of Chemical Education* 68: 148–49.

———. 1994. "Probing Student Misconceptions in Thermodynamics with In-Class Writing." *Journal of Chemical Education* 71: 1056–57.

Borasi, R. and B. J. Rose. 1989. "Journal Writing and Mathematics Instruction," *Educational Studies in Mathematics* 20: 347–65.

Diab, S. M. and R. Kloser. 1996. "Journals, Attitudes, and Performance," In *The Teaching Professor,* ed. Maryellen Weimer, 4 (November). Madison, WI: Magna Publications, Inc.

Felder, R. M. 1995. "A Longitudinal Study of Engineering Student Performance and Retention. Instructional Methods and Student Responses to Them." *Journal of Engineering Education* 84: 361.

Fulwiler, T. 1987. *The Journal Book.* Portsmouth, NH: Boynton/Cook Publishers.

Halsor, S. P. and P. B. Heaman. 1991. "Enhanced Student Learning through Writing in a Physical-Geology Class." *Journal of Geological Education* 39: 181–84.

Marwine, A. 1989. "Reflections on the Uses of Informal Writing." In *Writing to Learn Mathematics and Science,* eds. P. Connolly and T. Vilardi, 56–69. New York: Teachers College Press.

Selfe, C. L. and F. Arbabi. 1983. "Writing to Learn: Engineering Student Journals." *Engineering Education* 74: 86.

Schulz, K. H. and D. K. Ludlow. 1993. "Using Writing-to-Learn Assignments in Chemical Engineering Courses." Proceedings of the ASEE Annual Conference, Urbana-Champaign, IL, 776–79.

5

Designing Conversations
The Journal in an Engineering Design Class

Joel Greenstein, Ph.D., and Beth Daniell, Ph.D.

I tended to use my out-of-class responses as a time to ask questions. Looking back through all of them, I found *lots* of question marks, with lots of answers from you!

from Scot's journal

Joel, an industrial engineer, teaches a graduate course on engineering design. The objective of the course is to help students learn to create products that are useful, usable, and liked by their users. Shortly before he began teaching the course, Joel attended two Writing-Across-the-Curriculum (WAC) workshops on the Clemson campus. These experiences persuaded him to integrate into the course a journal in which students would respond to the class readings, reflect on class discussions, and develop ideas for their projects. He hoped that keeping a journal would motivate his students to keep up with the course reading, lecture, and discussion. He wondered with Beth, a professor in English he'd met in the WAC workshops, how they might investigate whether the journal was accomplishing his goals.

To gain insight into the students' response to the journal, we analyzed what students said in journal summaries they wrote at the end of the course.[1] In this chapter we discuss the results of our analysis of the journal summaries from three successive offerings of the course. We provide evidence that the journal assignment, in addition to serving its intended pedagogical function, also served a rhetorical function—helping students modify their perceptions of the engineering design process. We also show how, as we attempted to enhance the students' acquisition of knowledge and skills in the course, our approach to the journal assignment moved from expressivist, to cognitive, to social.

The Initial Expressive Journal

The initial assignment for the journal was spare and open-ended: "Write a page responding to the reading assignment for each day." At the end of the semester, we used language about as spare and open-ended to ask students to write a two-page summary of their journals. Borrowing an assignment from Fulwiler (1989, 26), we asked them to discuss their growth and their problems in the course as evidenced in their journals. The responses varied wildly. Some students simply summarized the course texts. Some wrote about the course in general, but others told us that the journals and the discussions generated by them had helped them learn. Some wrote that class discussions, typically based on the journal entries, helped them learn the concepts of the course. Several students talked about the discussions as a means of learning from a variety of opinions. One student, Ken, stated, "Conflicting views were expressed on some issues and new insights were developed which made me question my previous point of view." Such comments, we believe, indicated that our pedagogical purposes were being fulfilled. Joel wanted students to consider a number of points of view and then make their own decisions, something not always easy to accomplish when the professor's voice is the only one that is heard.

Very few students admitted liking the writing, but several did confess that the journal assignment was useful. One complained that it was time-consuming, but then admitted that it "contributed to my better understanding of this course as a whole." For Pam, the journal was a "chore," but she found that reviewing her journal at the end of the semester "helped bring the course into focus." James wrote, "This habit of journal writing has helped me to put down my thoughts on paper, which would have otherwise gone unnoticed. It has also gone to improve my thought process as I can link up my thoughts in a chain, by referencing previous entries."

In their journal summaries students revealed that the journal assignment also served a rhetorical function—persuading students that looking at engineering design from the user's and customer's points of view is valuable. Most students come to such a design course with technical expertise but with little sensitivity for the needs of the human beings who will interact with their designs. To focus the design process on the needs of the user and customer rather than on the capabilities of technology requires a change in mindset, one often resisted by engineers.

We were surprised to find that the journals helped to change their minds. Journals actually gave the students a place to think through their objections to the principles of user-centered design, allowing them to convince themselves of the value of these principles. The journal was a place where it was all right to disagree with the texts; indeed using the journal to question and challenge the readings earned praise from the instructor. The journal—like Edison's notebooks (see Young 1994b, 13–14) or Chomsky's dissertation (quoted in Elbow 1987, 60)—was a place to work ideas out for oneself at one's own pace, coming to a personal synthesis of technological expertise and user-centered approach.

We found many comments in the journal summaries that seem like testimony to the belief that user-centered design is central to good engineering. Indeed, a conversion experience showed up fairly often in the journal summaries: Jerry actually called himself "a born-again industrial engineer." Another student, Kai, admitted: "I initially had a large amount of reserve to this 'design for usability' issue, but I now see it as the only way to design. It almost ensures success for a design." Finally, Don ended his journal summary by saying, "I went from skeptic to supporter of design for the user." Students often attributed this change in their attitudes directly to class discussion, but we believe that class discussion was powerful because it came after students had had a chance to write out their quarrels with this perspective.

Looking back on the initial journal assignment, it now seems clear that Joel took an expressivist approach to journal writing. The open-endedness and informality of the journal and journal summary assignments and the emphasis on growth in the journal summary assignment are certainly hallmarks of an expressivist pedagogy. True, the original purpose of the journal was to provide students a place to work out problems and an incentive to keep up with the readings, but it had another function we see now: It gave students a place to be spontaneous and original. Joel's expressivist orientation makes sense, for his introduction to Writing-Across-the-Curriculum and journal writing came first from Art Young, whose pedagogy Faigley has classified as expressivist (Faigley 1986, 531, note 3). Indeed, it is surprising that we weren't confronted with even more resistance from engineers trained to rely on hard data, to expect precision and exactness, and to discount personal feelings. But perhaps this clash of cultures makes it understandable that even while students listed benefits of the journal and the class discussion based on it, they also expressed real antipathy for this assignment. And, of course, some students resisted the journal and the journal summary assignments by writing responses that were so perfunctory as to be virtually nonexistent.

Increasing the Emphasis on Writing to Learn

The next year, relying on the response of students from the preceding year as well as our own perceptions, we introduced some additional changes in the journal assignment to make more explicit our purposes in making the assignment and our expectations regarding the content. Wanting more students to use the journal as a tool for learning, we distributed an additional two-page handout on the use and evaluation of journals, which we borrowed from Lex Runciman (see Appendix at the end of this chapter). No longer did we have a spare and open-ended assignment; this time we included not only more explanation of the assignment and more direction, but also more explicit commentary on the evaluation of the journals. Because a number of students in the preceding class had used the journal entries to respond superficially and the journal summaries merely to summarize the two course texts, we asked for more reflection on their learning. To this end, when we made the journal summary assignment at the end of the semester, we gave students a list of the kinds of thinking journals encourage, which we gleaned from Fulwiler's essay "Responding to Student Journals." Since we were clear this time about what we wanted, students gave us examples of observation, speculation, confirmation, doubt, questions, self-awareness, connections, digression, dialogue, information, revision, and posing and solving problems (1982b, 164–68).

We again saw evidence that the journal had served rhetorical and pedagogical functions. Once again we found the conversion experience. One student said that class discussion was a factor in "converting" him to user-centered design. Another student, Josh, said he was "converted to human factors," citing the crash of an Indian Airbus that semester arising from a design-induced pilot error. Another talked of "feeling cheated in my education because we had not stressed these topics in any of my undergraduate courses."

About the journal as a teaching tool, Kathy commented, "The writing prepared me for class discussion," while another student argued that the journal "compensated for not talking" during class discussion. Students also mentioned two social benefits of the journal: It increased their involvement with the class and their interaction with Joel. This sort of interaction positively influences learning because, as Vygotsky explains, working with a peer who might be somewhat ahead on a developmental task or with an interested instructor allows students of any age, not just children, to reach their "zone of proximal development"—the place where individuals perform tasks with others that they are not ready to perform alone (1978, 86–88).

As before, students reported in their journal summaries that they didn't like the journal assignment at first, but they then went on to enumerate its benefits. The benefits noted by our students are consistent with those reported by Fulwiler (1982a) on journals in general and by Selfe and Arbabi (1983) and by Rumpf, Melachrinoudis, and Mehra (1988) on journals in engineering classes. Our refined journal summary assignment asked students to look specifically for evidence of the practice of the cognitive skills Fulwiler says occurs in journals. In response, students supplied a good deal of such evidence. We cannot say for sure that the new journal assignment encouraged students to make more frequent use of these skills, as we intended. Perhaps the refined journal summary assignment simply helped students do a better job of reporting their use of these skills. We have grouped below their comments having to do with the cognitive benefits of the journal.

Thinking

Several students reported that the journal assignment gave them time to think or improved their thinking. They mentioned that the journal helped them remember the course material, organize their thoughts, and "clarify concepts." One man said that he became so used to this mode of thinking and responding that he was now keeping paper in both his living room and kitchen. Paying attention to the instructions for the journal summary, many students listed various modes of thinking—such as observation, digressions, and questions—that they had found in their journals, sometimes citing examples. Kelly commented, "I was surprised to find an example of each of the twelve ways of thinking the journal is supposed to encourage."

Growth

Several students discussed the journal as a record of their growth. One ranked the kinds of thinking listed in the journal summary assignment, saying that at first he used his journal only for "information," but later he used it for "discussion, doubts, thoughts, and confusing questions." Ryugi said that the journal allowed him to track the changes in his conceptual concerns—"from general concerns to more specific ideas and back again to general." Another student saw it as a record of his creativity: "Before the journal, many good ideas would fade away and be forgotten." Julia seemed pleased that toward the end her entries "reflect some confidence with the material."

Connections

Several students noted in their summaries that the journals gave them the chance to connect the course work or the readings with their own experiences. One man said that he liked the parts of his journal where he related design to experiences outside the course, like the baking pan that didn't fit in his oven. Another discussed his entry on the faults of a particular word processing program. Still another pointed to a long discussion in his journal about the ethics of "bad" design—designing to meet the customer's demands when they conflict with the user's needs.

Improved Writing

In contrast to the preceding year, several students remarked on improvement in their writing. Colby said, "I didn't think I had it in me to write this much. It helped my writing skills. As a result, my projects for other classes were of better quality." Another said that the question he prepared for class "would become an essay as I tried to answer it myself." Another man said that he had become a better writer because until he worked on this journal, the only kind of writing he had done was the formal academic essay. Several others mentioned the journal's expressive function, noting, for example, the opportunities it gave them to discuss their personal opinions.

Reading

In the summaries several students remarked that the journal requirement helped them complete readings on time. Others talked about the effect of the journal on their reading. One said that keeping the journal "improved the way I read," though he didn't explain how. Andrew reported that the review of his journal showed that as the semester progressed he became more critical of what he read: "Toward the end I would question the authors." This student continued: "As a result, I think I understood what I was reading more than I would have if I did not have to keep the journal."

Increasing the Emphasis on Collaborative Learning

Because of enrollments of more than forty in each of the two previous years, in the third year we made more changes in the journal assignment. Using Beth's approach to journal writing in her graduate composition theory course, we asked the students to bring to class a typed one-page journal response to the reading, rather than longhand entries in a notebook. The handout explaining the use and evaluation of journal writing remained essentially the same, and the journal summary assignment continued unchanged.

The intent of the changes to the journal assignment was to enhance the students' out-of-class responses as a tool for collaborative learning. The responses continued to serve as a basis for individualized learning through writing; they continued the expressive and cognitive functions of the journals. But in their new typed, one-page format, the journal responses could be used much more actively and directly in class as the basis for collaborative learning, both in small groups and as a class. Joel would also be able to collect and respond to these typed one-page responses much more conveniently than to the handwritten responses in forty or more spiral-bound notebooks.

With the new format Joel often began class by asking students to exchange and read each other's responses in small groups and then to discuss the similarities and differences. This exercise served at least three worthwhile purposes. First, students could refresh their memories of the day's material more quickly than Joel could have by presenting his own overview in lecture form. Second, exchanged entries exposed students to insights gleaned by other students from the reading. And, third, students could hear informal responses to their ideas from a few of their peers. Joel could then bring the students together to discuss as a class what the small group discussions had identified as key topics or issues deserving further discussion. Used this way, the journals were no longer just individual writings; they had now become class texts, to be shared, commented on, and modified by other students.

At the end of the class period, Joel collected the responses. Prior to the next class meeting, he scanned each response and entered a brief comment of his own on the student's paper. For example, he might indicate his agreement or disagreement with the opinions expressed by the student. He might clarify a difficult concept for a student. Or he might introduce the student to a point of view different from the one presented in the assigned reading. These papers were returned to the students at the beginning of the next class. In this way, Joel maintained a dialogue with each student through the entire course.

As in previous years, journal summaries supported our perceptions that the journal assignment served pedagogical and rhetorical purposes. With respect to pedagogy, one student wrote, "I can confidently say that these writings stimulated my thinking. I could draw connections between one reading and another and could relate the topic under discussion to my personal experiences. The writings also improved my awareness. I have asked myself many questions in the writings." Scot, whose quote heads the beginning of the chapter, said, "I easily made connections between the reading and my life. I wrote one whole paper on my problems with a door!" Michael wrote in his summary, "Another area I improved in as a result of these out-of-class writings was my reading ability. I learned how to be a more critical reader. I learned to stop when I read something interesting and really consider it. When I actually did that, I was able to get more out of the reading than the author even presented."

Other students also commented, though more briefly, on the improvement they saw in their thinking and writing. One said, "I saw an improvement in the way I wrote my responses day to day." Another, "The out-of-class writings gave me many opportunities to improve my thinking and writing skills."

Once again students used their journal summaries to report how their writings indicated a change in their thinking about design. Garrett commented, "When examining the out-of-class and the in-class writings over the last four months, I could tell that my views about design had 'softened' over the course of the semester." Another said, "My writings have evolved from a more skeptical viewpoint to an advocacy of the principles posed by the authors of the texts in the course." One student concluded, "Overall, I think the most important thing I have learned this semester is that as design engineers, we must never forget the human involved with the end design."

We looked for evidence in the journal summaries that the change to typed one-page responses used directly in class and returned quickly with comments served to enhance collaborative learning among the students and dialogue with Joel. We found evidence for these hypotheses. One student wrote, "During several writings, I seemed to dwell on specific points too much, but the discussion of the material in class seemed to direct my understanding of the material in the correct direction." Menard, who had worked as a design engineer for several years before returning to school to do graduate study, remarked,

> Perhaps I had an advantage over most of the class in understanding design methods, since I have designed in the past. This could have polarized my opinions, but the views of others in class were thought provoking. After working with my design team and using the feedback from the out-of-class writings, I started to write like I did before Technical Writing 101 and working for 5 years.

Finally, Scot observed,

> I tended to use my out-of-class responses as a time to ask questions. Looking back through all of them, I found *lots* of question marks, with lots of answers from you! Your answers, I believe, helped me understand and/or pointed out things that I obviously missed in the readings. I learned how to read the chapters and obtain more information just by knowing how you would respond to my writings.

When we changed the format of the assignment—how it looked on the page and how the text was handled after it was written—other changes occurred: in the quality of the writings themselves and in the content of the student commentary on them. Joel believes that, overall, the journal response papers and the class discussions based on them were of better quality—more insightful, more reflective—than those of the previous two years. We think that part of the reason is that the journal response paper became, in this third year, a public genre, a response to be read not just by the instructor but by an audience of one's peers as well. This format allowed students to see other papers and compare their efforts to those of others. The student papers became both textual and conceptual models. A given student's ideas were commented on and questioned by other people who had just read the same material. It's one thing to hand in sloppy work to a professor, but quite another to offer it to one's peers in a public performance.

In addition, another important change in the assignment that contributed to improving the quality of out-of-class writings was that Joel provided more feedback more often. Previously, Joel had been able to respond to the spiral-bound journals only two or three times during the semester. But with the typed one-page responses, he found he could immediately steer people who seemed to have gotten lost back on track. He could point to an alternative theory, ask them to reread a passage, correct a misunderstanding, or recognize good ideas by writing in the margins, "Yes" or "Precisely!"

Because students received immediate feedback, they learned sooner rather than later what Joel expected, not only in terms of the journal but also in terms of the quality of the work. The superiority of the journals in this third year convinced us that while journals are valuable as expressive and thinking tools, their value can increase substantially when they are used socially. When journals are used in classroom discussion and when they are responded to quickly, they become an even more powerful means to learning.

Orienting Students to Professional Practice

Joel's original intention in using journal-writing techniques was to help students learn engineering design. If the journal summaries are valid at all as a window on student thinking, then the journal assignment has indeed served this function. Not only do the students learn the technical material because they have to struggle with it—explain it, question it, relate it—but they also learn other skills. Students have become, by their own testimony, better writers, better readers, better thinkers, better contributors to their teams, and better speakers. All of these skills—from using technology, to applying design methodologies, to problem solving, to speaking in a more confident manner in both small and large groups—enhance students' professionalism.

The comments of the students in their journal summaries provide explicit evidence that their journal writing oriented them to professional engineering practice. In the first year one man, already working as an engineering manager in a nearby firm, remarked on our journal summary assignment: "The comment concerning 'seeing growth' in the journal entries has helped clarify the form of the journal that will be useful to me. My new approach will be to limit entries to facts, ideas, thoughts, and observations that document my growth as a manufacturing engineer." The next year, two students specifically noted that the journal had helped them carry out design methodologies in their team projects; another reported that notes of class discussion in the journal helped resolve disputes that arose among team members during work on the projects. One man said that keeping the journal "gave me confidence for discussion." In the third year one student wrote at some length about how the journal assignment oriented him to the practice of his profession:

> I found myself, as the semester progressed, being able to relate what I read about every night to what I was doing in my project team, what I had done in projects in the past, and even what I can do in projects in the future. The last, being able to apply what I have learned, is the most important to me. Throughout my responses, I got better and better at not only relating what I have read, but telling how I can use what I read in the future.

We believe that the multiplicity of perspectives we encouraged through journal writing is particularly suitable to the learning of engineering design. A lecture-oriented class tends to convey the notion that the approach or approaches presented by the professor are the only acceptable ways to design when, in fact, there is seldom one right design or one right way to approach a design problem. A participatory approach is particularly suited to engineering design because it models the communication—writing and speaking—that takes place in the practice of engineering design, itself a participatory process involving the written and oral contributions of a number of people with various perspectives and areas of expertise. Both the journal writing and the class discussion based on the writing serve this purpose: Students articulate their views, problems, and concerns, and then these are discussed in both small and large groups.

All of this Joel intended consciously. What he did not intend, at least not consciously, was to "convert" students to his way of seeing design. He didn't feel that he needed to; after all, they would have to know the material to pass the course. But what has happened is that the journal has become the place where students argue about the value of using user-centered approaches to engineering design. Their resistance is not resisted but instead allowed to run its course. In the end, the students convince themselves.

Some Final Thoughts

When we decided to analyze the journal assignments by comparing and contrasting the responses in the journal summaries, Beth saw a progression easily described in terms from composition theory: Our initial journal assignment reflected an expressivist approach; after our first revision, the journal assignment came to mirror a cognitive perspective; in the third year, it took a more social bent. This was not something we had planned. The changes we made in the journals had seemed to us to be responses to pragmatic problems—superficial work by students one year, too many students the next. First, we wanted students to be more reflective in their journals, to be more aware of using journal writing as a way to look at their own thinking. Then we wanted to make it possible for students to get more feedback more often, something that was difficult to do with the large classes. But what happened is that the journal and the course itself shifted from an individual model of learning to a social model of learning. Young argues that this is what has happened with Writing-Across-the-Curriculum theory and practice generally (1994a, 60).

Interestingly, the journal summaries in the third year exhibited much more technical detail than summaries in the previous years. Students wrote animatedly about cross-functional design teams; product development cycle times; integrated product development methodologies; life-cycle design; testable design specifications; rapid prototyping; iterative design and testing; the value of affordances, constraints, and feedback to the user; and the danger of creeping featurism for the designer. In the first two years, there was only a rare comment in the journal summaries that Beth, a nonengineer, couldn't follow. In the third year, she was astounded at how much technical information the students wove into their discussions of their learning, writing, and reading. We believe the writing in the course had ceased to be something separate from the knowledge made and conveyed in the course. Instead, the journal became one of the vehicles for constructing the knowledge in the course. Other evidence of the journal's full integration into the course came from the lack of comments in the journal summaries about what a chore journal writing was. The journal had finally become part of the conversation of engineering design.

Notes

1. The journal summaries used throughout this chapter were collected over several years, and the authors were not aware of the identities of individual student writers. In an attempt to make the use of student samples similar to those in other chapters, the editors have inserted fictional names for many of the quotes in this chapter.

Works Cited

Elbow, P. 1987. "Closing My Eyes as I Speak: An Argument for Ignoring Audience." *College English* 49 (January): 50–69.

Faigley, L. 1986. "Competing Theories of Process: A Critique and a Proposal." *College English* 48 (October): 527–42.

Fulwiler, T. 1982a. "The Personal Connection: Journal Writing Across the Curriculum." In *Language Connections: Writing and Reading Across the Curriculum,* eds. T. Fulwiler and A. Young, 15–31. Urbana, IL: National Council of Teachers of English.

———. 1982b. "Responding to Student Journals." In *Writing and Response: Theory, Practice, and Research,* ed. C. M. Anson, 149–73. Urbana, IL: National Council of Teachers of English.

———. 1989. "Journal Writing." In *Reading, Writing, and the Study of Literature,* eds. A. W. Biddle and T. Fulwiler, 135–61. New York: Random House.

Kempf, D. L., E. Melachrinoudis, and S. Mehra. 1988. "Student Journals in Engineering Education: Do They Work?" *Engineering Education* 78 (February): 313–16.

Runciman, L. Unpublished class material. Linfield College. McMinnville, OR.

Selfe, C. L. and F. Arbabi. 1983. "Writing to Learn: Engineering Student Journals." *Engineering Education* 74 (November): 86–90.

Vygotsky, L. S. 1978. *Mind in Society: The Development of Higher Psychological Processes,* eds. M. Cole, V. John-Steiner, S. Scribner, and E. Souberman. Cambridge: Harvard University Press.

Young, A. 1994a. "The Wonder of Writing Across the Curriculum." *Language and Learning Across the Disciplines* 1 (January): 58–71.

———. 1994b. *Writing Across the Curriculum.* Blair Resources for Teaching Writing. Englewood Cliffs, NJ: Prentice-Hall.

Appendix

Lex Runciman's Generic Journal Description for Students

One of your central learning activities this term will be keeping a journal. You should think of this writing as talking out loud or thinking out loud. And you should realize that some of your most interesting (to you, I mean) and productive journal entries may well begin with questions or notions that you haven't really thought about much.

If you're used to writing essays and tests only, then you'll need to lower your standards in order to get the full benefits of your journal. Think about it: Essays and tests ask you to be sure. They ask you to write clearly and authoritatively about a topic that you've come to some conclusions about (or even mastered). Part of the challenge of writing essays and tests lies in deciding for yourself what your conclusions are. No doubt you will come to conclusions this term, and you can certainly use your journal to reflect them and examine them. But you can and should also use the journal to try out new ideas, to pick up on some aspect of class discussion that you disagreed with or agreed with or that we didn't get to fully air. The journal can and should be your place to continue our class discussions. It can and should be your place to record your reactions to the reading you do. Your entries can agree with the reading, question it, argue with it, or just talk about what might be confusing. If you end up temporarily lost or at a dead end, that's reasonable and even useful. The point is that you're using the journal to become involved in the issues the course raises. And don't forget to go back and reread earlier entries; sometimes they'll still look accurate, sometimes they'll look naive, and sometimes you'll find that you now have answers to earlier questions. These insights can become new entries.

Finally, use your journal to draw connections between this course and others you've had. Education is more than a menu of courses; education is often the links you find between them.

How Will Journals Be Graded?

The journal counts as 20% of your grade, and it will be evaluated according to three criteria: commitment, ambition, and engagement. Your journals will *not* be graded according to correctness or paragraphing or sentence structure. So feel free to write quickly. Punctuate in any way that makes sense at the time.

You will be asked to evaluate your own journals once at midterm and again at the end. Both times, an evaluation sheet will be provided. You'll see that this sheet gives descriptions of an "A" journal, a "C" journal, and an "F" journal; "Bs" and "Ds" fall somewhere in between. You'll be asked to evaluate your journal according to each criterion, using two or three sentences to explain your evaluation, and you'll then arrive at an overall grade. *At midterm, turn in your evaluation sheet with six copied pages of your journal; at the end of the term, I'll want your evaluation together with twelve copied pages.* Choose your pages so that they support your evaluation. I will read your evaluation, look at your supporting pages, and decide whether or not your evaluation seems reasonable. If I see some problem, I will ask for your entire journal.

Journal Evaluation Sheet

An "A" journal	A "C"	An "F"

COMMITMENT

Shows regular and frequent entries—averaging 4 or more per week. Entries themselves are provocative, spirited, lively, and quite various. Entries may vary quite widely in length, but they regularly go on for some time (more than a page) in order to reflect and accommodate extended thought.

Regular, but less frequent entries—3 per week average. Entries themselves sometimes lively and spirited, sometimes a little tired or flat. Entries occasionally lengthy and complicated, but often brief, sometimes sketchy.

Entries irregular, with noticeable time gaps between them. Or entries tend to bunch up, with perhaps two or three in a week, then no more for a week or ten days. Overall, fewer than 3 entries per week. Entries rarely lengthy, usually brief, often fragmentary.

AMBITION

Entries regularly try to stretch or to pose questions that engage the writer, but for which the writer may have no ready answer. Entries willing to speculate, and willing to try to make connections between this course and other courses. Entries show the writer willing and eager to draw connections between course material and the writer's lived experience. Writer is clearly trying to get as much from the journal writing as possible.

Some entries willing to pose questions or to speculate. But most entries discuss conclusions rather than reach for them. A few entries will try for connections outside the course, and some entries may include the writer's lived experience.

Entries seem cursory, the result of coercion rather than interest. Little or no effort to speculate or to reach for more than obvious conclusions. Little or no attempt to connect to other courses or life outside this class.

ENGAGEMENT

Entries show that this writer has regularly reread earlier entries to comment on them, contradict them, or to find some order in them. Over time, the journal evolves a set of questions or issues or concerns which are specific to this writer, and specific journal entries identify and explore these issues.

An occasional entry shows that the writer has reread earlier entries or has returned to earlier questions or issues. But overall, the journal gives only an intermittent sense of progress or of deepening understanding.

Little or no evidence that this writer has reread earlier entries. Little or no sense of progress or deepening understanding. Little or no sense that this writer has reflected on much beyond the immediate entry.

6

Using Journals in Computer Science Courses
Helping Students Connect

Bobbie Othmer, Ph.D., and Terry Scott, Ph.D.

Today we went over another example of the Pencil and Paper Computer. This was about reading 2 integers and multiplying them and "outputting" (is this a word?) the result. In the example done in class, a loop was used. A loop is a way to repeat a set of commands. In training my dog, for example, I have been told that it is important to repeat a lesson three times at a session. If I was a computer, this would be an appropriate place for a loop. (Likewise, I am programming my dog!)

Anneliese in CS-101,
Introduction to
Computer Science

Need for Good Communication Skills

Computer scientists are in a profession that demands good problem-solving skills, the ability to handle large amounts of detail, the ability to learn about new developments in technologies and methodologies, and an awareness of the social effects of their work. But it is not enough to possess these skills and knowledge—it is also important to be able to communicate their knowledge in writing to others. Computer scientists have the same needs for communication skills as other professionals. In particular, they need good writing skills to write reports, documentation, proposals, recommendations, and memoranda.

Computer science students are frequently not natural writers; some are actually very negative about writing. One way to help computer science students practice their writing is to have them take separate technical writing or advanced composition courses in English or technical communications departments. A current trend is incorporating writing assignments into computer science courses. Bickerstaff and Kaufman (1992), Curl (1992), Hafen (1994), Jackowitz et al. (1990), and Pesante (1991) all describe how to do this. Often these integral writing assignments take the form of polished term papers or projects that take a great deal of time for students to complete and for teachers to evaluate.

Formal writing is not only time-consuming, it is also somewhat narrow in scope since major projects focus on just one aspect of a topic. Computer science teachers worry, then, about sacrificing coverage of content to the needs of longer, more formal writing assignments. Journal writing—an informal but sustained writing activity often seen as using writing to learn—can provide a solution to adding more writing into the computer science curriculum while ensuring content is also learned.

Why Journals in Computer Science?

While the most compelling motivation for using journals in computer science classes is to help students learn the material, other important factors include the need for more writing by computer science students, preparation for professionalism, and lifelong learning. The journal serves a practical method for teaching nontechnical subject matter.

Journals Encourage Learning Course Content

As teachers of computer science, we want to encourage active and deep learning by our students and improve their problem-solving capabilities. The use of journals can help achieve these goals. Students learn the subject matter as well as how to think about it. Writing in a journal provides an opportunity for students to make connections between new knowledge and their prior knowledge and experience; to make new knowledge personal; and to reflect on processes, meaning, and connections. This kind of writing involves the student in both active and deep processes of learning and critical thinking. Without this kind of questioning and responding, information from the instructor and texts may be stored away undigested and unprocessed, and thus not in a form that can be retrieved and applied in appropriate situations.

Journals Promote Problem Solving

Most computer science students are not used to writing as a method of problem solving or as a way of exploring or recording ideas, new information, and processes. When students write about a problem in an exploratory way, they generate ideas related to solving the problem. They also record their thinking processes and strategies as they solve a problem. This helps them become more aware of their thought processes. Skills learned keeping a journal can help students learn on their own when they are out of school; journals can also be useful for keeping track of data, processes, and information on the job.

Journals Help Students Keep Current in Their Field

Since computer science students need to keep up with developments in their field of study, writing shorter journal entries can be preferable to writing one long term paper during a course. Instead of one formal writing assignment reporting on one development, they can do several journal entries on different developments. Multiple journal entries encourage students to read more and to look for more articles and information.

Journals Provide Opportunities for Reflection on Ethics

More and more computer science educators are trying to include material on the social and ethical context of computer science in their courses. If we want this material to make a difference, we know students need to do more than just hear or read about ethical issues. One way to get them more involved is to require them to *write* about the material. Formal writing assignments are time-consuming for both student and instructor. Journal writing allows for reflection on complex issues involved in social or ethical situations, and the instructor's response—providing an important dialogue. Being informal, journal writing also encourages personal reflection, providing a place to really grapple with the issues so a person can see what she thinks or believes.

Journals Promote Writing Fluency

Journals provide opportunities for students to develop fluency without being overly concerned about the mechanics and requirements of formal writing. Journals help increase writing fluency in all students just through the practice of putting concepts and thoughts into written English. Students whose first language is not English can experience a marked improvement in fluency of English expression, when journals are used frequently enough.

Real improvement in writing skills requires that someone respond to writing issues like mechanics and organization. Writing improvement is best seen through multiple drafts of documents. However, journal writing provides a bridge to writing improvement because practice produces the facility necessary for more formal papers. Journal writing can also help students who are competent writers maintain their skills and increase their comfort level with using writing as a tool for learning.

How We Came to Use Journals in Our Computer Science Courses

Bobbie had heard a lot about Writing Across the Curriculum and how various writing activities could not only improve student writing but also improve learning. In particular, she read a lot about using a class journal. In *The Journal Book,* Grumbacher (1987) discussed the use of a journal with her high school physics students. She found that students became more aware of their problem-solving processes and used their journals to tie what they were learning to their experiences. In another chapter of *The Journal Book,* BeMiller (1987) used journals, which he called workbooks, in college mathematics classes. He found that students understood the problem-solving process and the concepts from their courses better than when using traditional teaching methods.

After reading and attending a workshop on journals, Bobbie decided to try journals in two upper division computer science classes: Operating Systems and Computer Architecture. She also had the encouragement of a very supportive writing coordinator.

Terry's first experience with using journals in a classroom was a gentle introduction. He used journals in an honors seminar entitled the Atomic Bomb. The course was team-taught with another instructor, John Bromley, who had taught English, Journalism, and Humanities classes for many years, using journals as a regular part of these classes. Reading the journals in the honors class as a team made it possible to share grading goals and standards. It also made it easier to see how to use comments to help the students. Once Terry had some experience, it was easy for him to try journals in his computer science courses.

What Bobbie Did with Journals

Bobbie wanted to see whether journals could be used effectively in a technical course such as Operating Systems or Computer Architecture. Although journals were used similarly in both technical courses, the description and examples that follow are from using journals in Computer Architecture. The goals of the journal in that course are

- to help students clarify concepts
- to help students actively respond to material read for class
- to help students remember and understand what they are reading
- to help students in problem solving
- to provide a forum for working on concepts where evaluation depends upon effort and quality of thought rather than getting the "right answer"
- to provide a forum in which to ask questions

- to collect thoughts about topics under discussion during the class session
- to report on outside reading
- to improve writing fluency

The text for the course is Patterson and Hennesey, *Computer Organization and Design: The Hardware/Software Interface.* Chapter 1 is an introduction to hardware. It also discusses the great strides made in the development of computer hardware and some of the history of computers. The purpose of the chapter is to set the stage for the rest of the material, while trying to engage the reader. In their journals students were asked to identify three things in Chapter 1 they found interesting and to write about why they were of interest. Having students focus on their own responses to the historical developments described improved motivation.

Chapter 2 is about defining and measuring computer-system performance. Particular performance problems were assigned and students were asked to state explicitly what was known, what was to be found, what formulas might apply, and to identify subgoals of the problem. This kind of entry helped students improve their problem-solving skills without being concerned about losing points for getting the wrong answers. The problems were corrected by Bobbie when she collected the journals, giving students needed feedback.

The students were then given an assignment where the answers needed to be correct. In his journal, Noel restated the parameters of the question and then answered the problem as follows:

Exercise 2.1:

A. What we want: A comparison of performance of two systems based on cost effectiveness. Which of two systems is most cost-effective in running program 1? How much more cost-effective is it?

B. What we know: Two systems are identified as S1 and S2. Two programs are identified as Program 1 (P1) and Program 2 (P2). S1 costs $10,000. S2 costs $15,000. P1 takes 10 seconds on S1 and 5 seconds on S2. Cost-effectiveness (CE) is the ratio of performance to cost. Performance (PF) is defined as the reciprocal of execution time (ET). (Execution time is in units: seconds/task, so performance is in units: task/seconds.)

C. Formulas that apply: $CE = PF/COST$, $PF = 1/ET$, $CE\ Ratio = CE_A/CE_B$
Answer: PF for S1 running P1 is $1/ET = 1/10 = .1$
              PF for S2 running P1 is $1/ET = 1/5 = .2$
Therefore S2 has higher performance.
CE for S1 running P1 $= 1/10 / 10,000 = 10 \times 10^{-6}$ (PF/COST)
CE for S2 running P1 $= 1/5 / 15,000 = 13.33 \times 10^{-6}$ (PF/COST)
Therefore S2 is more cost-effective than S1 (running P1)
              $13.33 \times 10^{-6}/10.00 \times 10^{-6} = 1.33$
so S2 is 1.33 times more cost-effective than S1

Another assigned journal entry involved assessing an advertisement for a computer in which it was claimed that the advertised system "clocks over 110 VAX MIPS." Students were asked to interpret what this statement meant and to discuss its validity. Their answers required applying concepts introduced in the chapter on performance to a real situation.

Chapter 3 of the text introduces the MIPS computer architecture as an example of a Reduced Instruction Set Computer (RISC) architecture. Four design principles are introduced. In their journals, students wrote about examples in the MIPS architecture that illustrate these four principles. This helped students connect the details of the MIPS instruction set with the designers' goals and with the principles behind RISC architecture.

Chapter 5 of the text describes the design of a simple processor. In a focused journal write students were asked to discuss the tradeoffs between added complexity in the control and datapath and the desire for optimal use of the space in the instruction set. Writing out their responses helped students understand the consequences of instruction set design decisions. Justin responded to the question as follows:

I found from the homework problems that for each additional instruction format the complexity of the datapaths and control units were increased. I had to add more datapaths and either change or add control lines. The more formats included the more complicated a datapath would get. This would lend itself to increasing the chances for error or problems occurring in datapaths. Adding formats do increase flexibility with more possibilities in instructions and less reliance on the base operations to create the same results. But with the added complexity and the stepping away from the simplicity of a reduced set the implementation and execution of instructions can be harder because more instructions are not of similar types. Many different sets of instruction formats require special consideration to run each set. With less instruction formats more instruction types can be similar reducing complexity which increases reliability and the efficiency of the hardware setups. More instructions can use the hardware if they are similar in type.

What Terry Did with Journals

Traditionally beginning computer science courses have been an introduction to computer programming. Recently some computer scientists have argued that the beginning course should offer a broad overview of the field of computer science. Terry has used journals in a breadth first computer science course on two different occasions, in a Pascal programming course for nonmajors once, and three different times in the Atomic Bomb class mentioned earlier. For all three courses, he found the feedback from students to be the strongest aspect of the journals. Even quiet students wrote helpful information. They talked about what they didn't understand, what was helpful to them, and what wasn't. After reading several journals, Terry knew pretty well how the class was going. With this kind of feedback, he could make changes to the way the class was taught while it was in progress. He also got to know the students better and sooner.

Terry also found new ways of looking at computer science concepts. For example, "The Paper and Pencil Computer" quoted at the beginning of the chapter was provided by the textbook as a very simple simulation of a computer that illustrates aspects of machine and assembly code. No multiplication operation was provided. In her journal, Anneliese related the loop to everyday life. Her quote that heads the chapter is such an example.

In another journal entry, Anneliese's understanding seemed to increase as she discusses how to convert number bases:

Today we reiterated Friday's lesson regarding binary, decimal, and hexadecimal representations and their conversions. Since doing the exercises assigned, I feel a little more comfortable with this. I'm still slow, but I do understand it.

A couple of points that I'd like to stress — that helped my understanding of these conversions' systems.

- To convert decimal to ANY base — divide by the base #, recording the remainders from R to L.
- The largest # allowable in n base is $n-1$.

Yet another important topic we touched on today: binary digit points, or bit points. These are equivalent to decimal points! Instead of tenths or 1/10, they are 1/2 or 1/16 — etc.

During the breadth first computer science class, students discussed aspects of computers in society. Terry brought in newspaper and magazine articles with current news topics for discussion. One of these articles described police cars being equipped with computers that could access the database of the stolen car. One concern of civil libertarians is the possibility that police might misuse this function by accessing the database more for minorities. In their journals students wrote extensively about their views on whether or not computer-equipped patrol cars were desirable.

Of course, the main reason Terry uses journals is to encourage the students to learn more about the content of the courses. By writing he hopes the students will think about the material outside of class and in a more active way and that this thinking will promote more learning. From his experience writing helps keep students focused on the class, which is necessary for learning to occur. Whether journal writing is the most effective way of maintaining this focus is not entirely clear.

Positive Outcomes of Using Journals

We have seen many positive outcomes from using journals in computer science courses including enhanced communication between students and instructor, more active learning by the students, more and better attempts at critical thinking and problem solving, and more writing by students.

Journals give the students another avenue to communicate with the instructor, providing a way to tell the instructor about their difficulties with the course material (either explicitly or implicitly), interests and questions about related course material, concerns about the way the course is being taught, or problems with another student. A journal is also a way for shy students to let the instructor know what they are thinking and how they are doing with the class. An example from Mike, a computer architecture student, is shown below.

> Bobbie: What is a good way to keep the terms like CPI, clock cycles, etc. straight? I find myself forgetting the definitions! This chapter has been a good one because I have learned some valuable techniques for comparison procedures.
>
> Mike

In class sessions it is very likely that Mike would never have asked for such help or volunteered his evaluation of the chapter. He simply didn't speak aloud like this in class.

For the instructor, journals provide a window into the minds of the students. Especially helpful are entries that provide feedback on how the course is going, what students do not understand, what they do not find interesting, and what pedagogy they do not find useful. Students are much more candid in their journals than they are in classroom discussions on many of these issues. The frequent two-way communication provided by journals also gives another way to communicate with individual students if there is a behavioral problem.

We have found the response of the instructor to individual entries can make students feel more valued. If students sometimes read their journal entries to the class or to a group of class members, or if references to journals are made to start a class or group discussion, then the journal can also increase communication among students in class.

Journal writing almost forces students to be active learners. Through their writing they overcome their natural passivity to just sit in class acquiring information. In addition to giving the student a question to actively grapple with in the journal outside of class, in-class journal writing can be used to provide material for a class discussion.

Issues about the social, ethical, or professional aspects of computing are often covered in computer science courses. However, teachers cannot assign the usual type of computer science problems which are highly technical to help students think through these issues. Journal writing, then, provides an opportunity for students to use the reading or lecture material on such topics and process it.

Since journal writing is informal and in some cases personal, it is a good method for students to explore aspects of ideas and follow their thoughts to a conclusion or solution. It also allows them to be more introspective about the problem-solving process and to take some intellectual risks without fear of being shot down. Since journals are not "finished" writing, students can explore issues without really having to get the right answer. They can enter into a conversation with the instructor about the subject matter almost without risk. Anneliese explored her thoughts and feelings about the widespread use of computers in the following entry from a CS-101 journal.

> Why is it that when I sit down at a computer I feel so removed from what I am doing? I'd like to air a complaint about the rush to apply computers to everything. I think that education has fallen prey to this. I'm having a hard time learning calculus with Mathematica. It's not that I mind using Mathematica. I just think that trying to relay calculus concepts via Mathematica frustrates me, more than anything. We do so much with graphs and calculations and we can only view a screen-full at a time. Often, a graph and its respective data table can't be viewed simultaneously. This is a problem when trying to understand what is happening. If I had it on paper, I could flip back and forth or see it all at once if I wanted to. And, there is a certain intimacy involved in paper and pencil that I don't feel at the computer. Punching keys and seeing numbers on a screen is different from writing the digits/calculations on paper. We have the sense of it coming from our fingertips to directly on the paper where our fingers are. Maybe my frustration comes from not adjusting well. But I think even some die-hard computer people would rather hold a book than read at a terminal. Any thoughts, Dr. Scott?

Finally, if used frequently enough, journal writing improves the writing fluency of students, especially those students whose first language is not English; it certainly causes students to spend more time writing. Ten to twenty-five percent of Bobbie's students are not native English speakers. Although writing in English is somewhat difficult and painful for these students, the practice at writing English in a relatively nonthreatening setting is especially useful for them.

How to Use Journals

Introducing the Journal Assignment

Concerns of an instructor starting to use a journal in a class include what to say in the initial assignment and explaining to students what they are supposed to do and why they are supposed to do it. Decisions must be made about how frequently the students should write in their journals, what kinds of things they should write about, and what the physical form of the journal should be.

Initially, it is important to explain the purpose of the journal in the course. The teacher also needs to discuss expectations and how the journal will be graded. The Appendix gives the complete journal assignment for Bobbie's computer architecture class.

If this is the students' first experience with a journal for a particular instructor, it is helpful to give an example of a good journal entry. Students appreciate a written description, which can also be put in a directory on a computer to which the students have access.

Specifying Physical Requirements

The physical format of the journal can be important to students. Spiral-bound notebooks have particular advantages. Since it is not easy to remove or add pages, students can look at their previous journal entries. If students have been working through certain problems, the instructor can see if progress is being made. On the other hand, a drawback of the spiral notebook is that students can't write in their journals while they are being responded to.

Bobbie prefers a loose-leaf notebook for journals. She only has to carry the most recent entries home to read, not a large pile of notebooks. Students can continue to work on their journals while the instructor is responding to earlier entries. Entries can be word processed, which is always nicer to read. Students can also submit entries via e-mail. The latter is especially attractive to computer science students who find electronic writing quite natural.

Detailing Frequency of Entries

The frequency of journal entries depends upon the purpose of the journal and the amount of other work that is assigned. If the journal is the main method students are using to learn the course material, they should write almost every day the class meets, either before or after each class. Writing should allow for continuity between entries, which is important for the class and the journal. Writing shouldn't be required so often, however, that it becomes a burden for the student or the instructor. If the journal is only a part of the work required for the class, teachers may make journal assignments less frequently; but if it is used too infrequently, some of the benefits of using a journal are lost.

Describing Content of Entries

What a teacher asks students to write about depends on what the instructor wants students to gain from the process. Terry has asked students to write about material in the book and lecture, which amounts to a kind of summary of the material. The journal then becomes a written outline of the course content. Again, students are more active learners using journals, but, for them to get the most out of journal writing, more than summarization should be required. If students can relate class material to personal experience or even material in other classes, then they will have thought more deeply about the information and the learning will be more complete.

Topics or questions asked in class can provide students with discussion points in their journal entries. Writing on a subject suggested in class, but not a part of the class lecture or the book, is a good activity for writing in journals. Students can also write a paragraph or two in class and hand it in or use it for discussion in small groups. These "directed writes" have many of the advantages of spontaneous journal entries.

In the Introduction to Computer Science class, the teacher brought in a newspaper article about two employees who were sending e-mail that said derogatory things about their boss. The e-mail was intercepted by the boss, read by him, and both employees were fired. Students were asked to discuss the whole situation in their journals. Points for them to consider included the right of privacy on a privately owned network, the morality of employees wasting company time, the morality of the boss reading the mail, and the use of encryption to protect the employees.

Students can also be asked to write about their process of solving a problem. The process of algorithm development requires students to come up with a step-by-step solution to a problem. Students must understand the problem, identify the inputs and outputs, identify the variables, and develop the steps for converting the input(s) to the output(s). If students are forced to write down each of these steps, the process of algorithm development will be thought out more deeply and, teachers hope, the process will become easier.

Collecting the Journals

It is important to collect and respond to journal entries frequently and promptly very early in the term, particularly for students who have had little or no experience with journal writing. If students are not writing often enough or are not following instructions in some other way, the mistake can be caught early and corrected. Collecting journals often also has the advantage that the reading of the journals isn't so big a chore. One way to avoid a huge rush of journals is to do the collecting on a rotating basis so that half the class is collected one week and the other half the following week. Collecting journals three or four times a term has proved beneficial for us. Teachers who collect less often than this find that reading journals becomes burdensome.

Responding to Journals

An issue that is separate from grading is responding to journals. The journals *must* be read. If teachers don't read the journals, students will generally do a poor job, and teachers may never know it. Without reading the journals, teachers lose the advantage of learning about the students, answering their questions, and all the other aspects that can make this activity a two-way communication channel. Most importantly, teachers lose the chance to learn from their students.

The process of reading is not enough, however; teachers need to show students that they read and value the writing. Answering questions, affirming what they write, and correcting them when they make mistakes show that the teacher is reading their work carefully. Because the journal should be for the students, it is important that teachers not be too critical in the grading of the entries. If students have to worry about correcting spelling errors, grammar, and other problems, they may be less at ease in the journal and reluctant to share their comprehension difficulties.

The correcting of factual mistakes should be undertaken, but this, again, should be done remembering journals belong to students and they are allowing you to read them. Rather than writing that a statement is wrong, teachers might give the correct information. The expression "Try to think of this in these terms . . ." provides an effective tone for a corrective comment.

Grading Journals

As with any assignment, students must know the grading criteria and method. One easy solution to grading the journals is to give them either a satisfactory or unsatisfactory. *Satisfactory* or *Unsatisfactory* can be given based on whether the journal was turned in and how often and how much was written. Bobbie uses a variation of the Satisfactory/Unsatisfactory grading scheme, but Terry believes it is important to recognize those students who have really worked at doing a good job. If the journal was maintained at the proper intervals and had sufficient writing, he awarded a minimum of a C/C+. Generally nothing was taken off for grammar, spelling, or other mechanical writing mistakes. He then looked to see how active the student had been in writing the journal to determine whether the grade should be higher than a C. He gave a C when the journal contained only a summary of the classroom lecture or the textbook. When students brought in additional material, asked good questions, gave new insights, or synthesized the material to draw conclusions, Terry awarded a grade of A or B.

Bobbie also uses a system of checks, with the option of giving a check minus or check plus. If the student has turned in all of the journals assigned with a grade of at least a check, Bobbie gives a grade of A− on the portion of homework represented by the journal. For this to work, the instructor must be diligent in monitoring journal entries for acceptability. The hope is that the students will find the journal a useful way to deal with learning course material and will be motivated by their usefulness rather than the grade.

Potential Problems and Solutions

Problems can occur when an instructor decides to use journals in class. The teacher may get less than the expected performance from students or may find an overload of work. It's also possible that journal writing may not be fully integrated into the rest of the class.

If students are not writing frequently enough, teachers might consider the workload for the class. If it seems reasonable, perhaps more frequent specific assignments will help. If students are not writing reflectively or deeply enough—or just not enough—perhaps they need examples of good journal writing to look at. Requiring that some entries be redone can help students understand what they should be doing or writing in class can help, especially if the instructor reads his own entry so students can see what he is looking for.

Sometimes the journal does not seem to add to the students' learning or to be very well connected to the class. If this is the case, teachers will want to reevaluate the type of writing to see if it meets their goals. Perhaps a different type of journal assignment may tie in better with the course material. For instance, if teachers expect students to create their own topics, perhaps a few specific topic assignments might help direct the writing better.

If instructors are having trouble keeping up with responding to journals, they can try several approaches. First the instructors should consider the work load. A journal should not be an "add-on"—that is, assigned on top of what is already a full load of homework. Instead, it should replace some of the work. If the class is too large to keep up with frequent journal entries, teachers might respond to only a portion of them. Entries can be chosen randomly, or students could indicate which ones they would like response to. Students could also respond to each other on occasion. Our experience is that journals should be used in only one class a semester, unless the instructor feels very confident about using them effectively and responding to them in a timely manner.

Keeping a journal is a semester-long assignment that takes planning and monitoring. If the first try does not live up to expectations, teachers may need to evaluate what worked and what did not, and then try again. It sometimes takes a few tries to get the assignment right, and some classes react more favorably to this kind of assignment than others.

A Final Comment

We have found that using journals in computer science classes can be very useful for both the students and the instructor in increasing communication, active learning, and critical thinking. A successful journal experience in a class requires planning and monitoring of the journal throughout the semester, but this care and effort can result in a richer learning experience by computer science students.

Works Cited

BeMiller, S. 1987. "The Mathematics Workbook." In *The Journal Book,* ed. Toby Fulwiler, pp. 359–66. Portsmouth, NH: Boynton/Cook.

Bickerstaff, D. D. and J. D. Kaufman. 1992. "Improving Student Writing Skills: Interdepartmental Collaborations." *SIGSCE Bulletin* 24, 1 (March): 42–45.

Curl, L. A. 1992. "Writing About Programming in CS1." *SIGSCE Bulletin* 24, 4 (December): 7–10.

Grumbacher, Judy. 1987. "How Writing Helps Physics Students Become Better Problem Solvers." In *The Journal Book,* ed. Toby Fulwiler, pp. 323–29. Portsmouth, NH: Boynton/Cook.

Hafen, M. 1994. "Developing Writing Skills in Computer Science Students." *SIGSCE Bulletin* 26, 1 (March): 268–70.

Jackowitz, P. M., R. M. Plishka, and J. R. Sidbury. 1990. "Teaching Writing and Research Skills in the Computer Science Curriculum." *SIGSCE Bulletin* 22, 1 (February): 212–15.

Pesante, L. H. 1991. "Integrating Writing into Computer Science Courses." *SIGSCE Bulletin* 23, 1 (March): 205–9.

Appendix

CMPT 342 Computer Architecture, Spring '97
Computer Architecture Journal

We will be keeping a journal for this class this semester. The journal is a place to record what you think about a topic, to respond to a reading, and to work with new concepts in a forum where effort and thought are more important than the "right answer."

The journal has several purposes including:

- to help you clarify concepts
- to help you actively respond to material you're reading
- to help you remember and understand what you are reading
- to help you in problem solving
- to provide a forum for working on concepts where the evaluation depends upon effort and quality of thought rather than getting the "right answer"
- to provide a forum in which to ask questions

- to use in class to collect thoughts about topics under discussion
- to improve your writing fluency

To include:

- responses or answers to assigned topics
- at least 8 responses to reading outside of the text
- thoughts stimulated by class activities, reading, etc.
- communications with the instructor

Journal Guidelines:

1. Keep your journal entries in a loose-leaf notebook or folder.

    If you are handwriting, write on ONE SIDE of the page only, legibly, and in ink or dark pencil. Word-processed journal entries are appreciated. You may also submit them via email to b-othmer@wcslc.edu

    Leave adequate margins—whether handwriting or word processing—for instructor's responses.

    Always date your journal entry and put your name on it before turning it in.

2. Remember, the primary audience for your journal is you, but your instructor will respond to your writing, and occasionally you will use your journal in class.

3. For the entries about readings from other sources than your text, find an article about computer architecture in a magazine, newspaper, journal, or on the net, and respond to some aspect of the article, either summarizing, explaining, drawing connections with what we are doing in class, criticizing, etc. Write 1–2 pages. Also hand in a copy of the article. Get at least two articles off the WWW. Turn in at least three of these by spring break, that is, by Feb. 23.

4. Journal entries are not formal writing such as is done when writing a paper or essay. Thus they do not need to be planned out ahead of time. Instead the entries should represent your thought on the subject.

5. Evaluation will be based upon writing a complete entry, turning it in on time, and evidence of some of the following strategies in the entry.

Strategies for Writing a Good Journal:

- *Write personally.* Be yourself. Use "I" references. Be honest about your responses to the texts, class activities, or discussions.
- *Write fully.* Say enough to explore your thoughts in some detail.
- *Do your best but don't obsess.* Punctuating and spelling correctly aid clear communication and make reading easier, but don't stifle your thinking by slavish attention to surface features.

- *Become engaged.* Move beyond summarizing. In exploring a topic, show you've done (or are doing!) some serious thinking about it.
- *Discuss details.* Mention specific ideas, passages in your text, images, etc. Include sketches and diagrams if these would help.
- *Make connections.* What have you seen that seems similar? What have you learned before that helps you understand some new idea? What personal experiences have you had that add to the interpretation and understanding of material in the text or other readings?

Grading:
I will collect entries at least weekly and read and respond to the entries and mark with a ✓, ✓+, or ✓−. If you have consistent checks on a sufficient number of entries all the way through the class, and do the final summary appropriately, you will receive 93% on the journal.

The journal will count 45% of your homework grade.

At the end of the semester we will organize, number pages, summarize, and turn in the entire journal for a final grade.

7

Electronic Journals
Encouraging Reflection in Preservice Teachers

MaryEllen Vogt, Ed.D., and Keith D. Vogt, M.S.

Hi! I had a wonderful last day with my students. I know you were right about remembering these kids as *our very first students.* . . . They were kind of like guinea pigs for us as we constantly experimented with new lessons and techniques to keep them interested in learning.

This quote is an excerpt from Muntzi's electronic journal written on her last day as a teacher-in-training. Following her formal university preparation, she entered the real world of the classroom where she completed her student teaching, one of the shortest apprenticeships of any major profession.

In some teacher-preparation programs, classroom experiences and course work begin early in the student's undergraduate career, while in others a fifth year of course work and classroom experience follows the awarding of a Baccalaureate degree. Throughout this preparation, preservice teachers are encouraged to reflect about their teaching, their students, their successes, and their failures. Often, though, few opportunities for this reflection really occur.

In this chapter, we introduce e-journals—electronic journals written by preservice teachers during their professional training. The e-journal entries described came from two very different contexts: one, a computer literacy course required of all elementary and secondary teacher candidates; the other resulted from student teaching. After analyzing and talking about our students' journals, we believe that e-journals provide new teachers with the opportunity to reflect on their teaching experiences in a supportive, nonthreatening environment.

Further, we think these kinds of reflections are critical to the development of effective teachers.

The New Teacher's Voice

Becoming a teacher is a challenging, difficult, and frequently exhausting experience. During teacher preparation, the preservice teacher, or teacher-in-training, often experiences feelings of inadequacy, worries about security and independence, and undergoes financial strain. As students move from the theoretical world of the university classroom to an actual teaching position, they can sense the dissonance between the ideal of the classroom and the realities they're experiencing. It is not uncommon, then, for new teachers to rely more on what appears to be the most expedient approach, rather than what is most effective and purposeful. Although undergraduate training is intended to prepare new teachers to be thoughtful, imaginative, empathetic, and creative, the preservice experience often creates new teachers who are, unfortunately, routinized and authoritarian (Casey 1989).

Providing a more meaningful learning experience for new teachers has meant finding ways to incorporate more self-reflection and self-evaluation into the teacher-preparation curriculum. This move has been a major departure from the traditional teacher-preparation model. The reflective practitioner model encourages students to focus on how they perceive their own teaching and how they might improve it. As university teachers, we have searched for concrete ways to help our students do this reflection about children, methods, materials, their belief systems, and teaching philosophy.

Our Experiences with Journals in Teacher Education

Prior to the advent of the Internet, we experimented in our university classes with using weekly journals to communicate with students in order to encourage reflection. In courses and during student teaching, preservice teachers wrote responses to open-ended questions and then submitted their journals during the following class or seminar. We responded to the entries with comments, suggestions, and insights. However, lag time between the preservice teacher's writing and receiving our responses, as well as infrequent face-to-face meetings, made it difficult to promote sustained reflection. Daily classroom or other field experiences could not be shared in this weekly format.

Additionally, our written comments on these traditional, once-a-week journals generally consisted of only one or two word responses within the text (e.g., "Interesting!" or "Frustrating, huh?") and three or four sentences at the end. While the opportunity existed for more extensive written responses, our comments were usually relatively brief.

With these traditional journals, the audience was also very limited: Only one person—the professor—read the students' writing and responded to questions or concerns. Other students and professors had no opportunity to respond unless the journal was passed around, and that kind of sharing would make public all previously written journal entries.

To address the lag time and the isolation just described, we have moved away from traditional journals and now use electronic journals, or e-journals. We have found that sending electronic journals shortens the time between students writing entries and their receiving responses from us, their university professors. Further, even though class still may only meet once or twice a week, e-journals increase contact with students to nearly a daily basis. The increased frequency of contacts, in turn, enables us to establish more personal relationships because we have immediate access to each other. Preservice teachers also seem to enjoy writing journals with each other, sometimes without our eyes or insights. Students reported they develop close relationships with classmates, another positive dimension to our using e-journals.

Research Support for Electronic Journals in Teacher Education

Although electronic journals are a relatively new addition to teacher-education programs and research on the effectiveness of this innovation is sparse, findings do support what we've experienced. McIntyre and Tlusty (1993) found preservice teachers are very receptive to using electronic journals, and computer access does affect the degree of their reflectivity. Not surprisingly, when students have their own computers at home, they are more likely to reflect on their teaching experiences than when they have to travel to a university computer lab to do their work.

Merseth (1990) found that beginning teachers who wrote electronic journals with other new teachers during their first year received a great deal of moral support from each other. Further, Casey and Roth (1992) found that when electronic journals were used during student teaching, teacher-professor contacts increased by nearly 90 percent, and professors and students reported relationships between them improved. These findings provided research support for our experiences: E-journals hold promise for improving the teacher preparation process, particularly encouraging student-professor relationships and student reflection.

Keith's Use of Electronic Journals in the Technology Methods Course

Keith teaches a technology class, Survey of Computer-Based Technology in Education, required of all elementary and secondary teacher candidates. He puts all information—the course syllabus, schedule, reading list with links, and software exercises—on the Internet. He creates a course website that all students have access to. Students are given e-mail accounts and are introduced to telecommunication in the first class session. The purpose of the course is to enable and encourage these future teachers to become computer-using educators who regularly and naturally use technological resources in their teaching.

After each class session, students are required to submit an electronic journal reflection on the class' activities. Keith responds within twenty-four hours to these e-journals, providing insights, asking questions, and clarifying issues. Students also respond to their readings online, and sometimes Keith inserts comments and questions directly into the text where students can then react to his comments. Occasionally, these conversations continue over several days. Students do exercises on various types of software online, and for the final exam they do a ten-minute presentation to the class using a presentation software.

Most of the students in the class have had no experience with computers and software. Many admit delaying the course primarily because of their fear of technology. In fact, during the first few sessions one semester, a woman literally cried most of the time. Though she said she had hated computers at the beginning, by the end of the course she had overcome this feeling and wrote frequent e-journal entries to Keith.

In surveys, students have indicated that approximately 20 percent are interested in the course content the first night; by the end of the semester, 90 percent report they value the use of technology in their own classrooms. Though encouraged to read their reading assignments directly online, many initially resist doing so and prefer to print the information onto a hard (paper) copy. By the last session, however, nearly all students are reading and writing journal entries online. Specific excerpts from their e-journals illustrate students' feelings about the process as well as their insights into the use of technology in teaching.

E-Journal Excerpts from the Technology Course

The following samples are taken directly from e-journals of students in multiple sections of the technology class. These samples were electronically and anonymously reproduced for research purposes. Many of the original dialogues between Keith and the students were lengthy, so for this chapter, these short excerpts include samples reflective in nature, whether positive or negative about the process of using e-journals:

> If I didn't have the pressure of this being a class for my credential, I might even be less stressed and more into just exploring the Internet!

> As was so well shown by the failure of earlier technologies to revolutionize education, I wonder how do we know this will be any different?

I am feeling anxious and elated at the same time about gaining access to increased computer skills. My innate resistance to new materials is disconcerting because of the levels of anxiety produced. . . .

I can't tell you how excited I am about learning a new program. I can use this program in the classroom for presentations. Now, I have to convince my principal to buy me a copy of all the software.

I have trouble comprehending the terminology. I hope that I do not ask too many questions. I am a little discouraged but I'll hang in there!

As some of the above samples show, even with the difficulties, the electronic journals have proven to be a very positive and central component of the course. Because e-journals allow two-way "conversations" often not possible in a class of thirty students, they enable Keith to know students on a far more personal level. Further, e-journals provide the chance to more fully address issues and concerns unique to individual students. Although Keith found the e-journals occasionally time-consuming, especially when entries were lengthy or conversations extended over several days, he believes in the value of this method of promoting thinking and reflection by preservice teachers. E-journals are definitely worth the extra effort.

MaryEllen's Use of Electronic Journals During Student Teaching

The context for MaryEllen's experience with e-journals is very different from Keith's. While many of his students were using technology for the first time, MaryEllen and her students were involved in a special project called Teacher-Net[1] at California State University, Long Beach. This project, originally funded by a grant, supplied student teachers with computers and modems along with training on how to access the Internet. In this project student teachers wrote e-journals to their university supervisor and to each other. They were required to send and receive e-mail journal messages at least five times per week during the fifteen weeks of student teaching. At present, all student teachers who participate in TeacherNet own their computers. Many enter student teaching with e-mail accounts and considerable Internet experience. Those without accounts are provided them at no cost through the university, and the university professors/supervisors provide training.

For research purposes, MaryEllen and her colleague Jean Casey (1994) examined more than 300 anonymously coded e-mail messages written by four groups of student teachers over the course of two semesters. In their analysis they found the comments fell into six categories, including reflections on the student-teaching experience: their students; classroom management and discipline; personal news; questions or concerns about technology; new teaching ideas or methods; and team building and support.

E-Journal Excerpts from Student Teaching

In analyzing the coded comments, MaryEllen and Jean realized that approximately one-third are reflective in nature. For example, student teachers frequently use their e-journals to describe specific incidents that have taken place at school, ask questions about the incidents, wonder about how effectively they handled them, and reflect about what they have learned from the experience. Some comments are positive and hopeful, while others clearly describe the challenges student teachers face.

One student described an incident to her supervising teacher as follows:

> I've learned that in order to try out some of my own ideas, I simply have to ask my master teacher. The two of us have very different styles, and at the beginning, I was so worried because I thought it would be difficult for me to grow. After the second week, I began to ask, very delicately I might add, if it would be all right if my group could begin working on a particular story. I also asked if I could begin having students write in a daily journal and use their invented spelling. She was very open to the idea and said she may even continue these activities after I'm gone!

Another student teacher described a common concern about classroom management:

> Today was better at school. I think that I may have some things put into a proper perspective. I had a meeting with the principal and the student who was defying and challenging me in front of the class on Wednesday. His contract was pulled so the next one means suspension. Ugghh. I'm just not this tough. Anyway, he passed the word onto his buddies and I guess they know I mean business . . . for this week, anyway. It's not too much fun for me or the other students though. I may write you again tomorrow, because I find some of this to be a bit of a mental release. I also want you to know what a challenge I am faced with.

Some of the e-journal entries deal with the student teacher's frustrations, insecurities, and self-doubt. Occasionally, these comments detail interactions with cooperating teachers or students. Other times, they appear to be reflections about teaching as a career choice. One student teacher, after an especially tiring and frustrating day in school, wrote the equivalent of a page of her worries and thoughts, and ended with, "Thanks for listening," an interesting choice of words for a *written* communication.

Other student teachers echo similar worries. For example, one wrote, "I'm sorry, but when I got into my shower this evening, I got really depressed. Is it something I'm not doing right? Do I need some child psychology classes or something? These children go beyond 'lively'—it seems they are just plain rude. I'm really questioning whether I have what it takes to be a teacher. Is it normal for me to feel this way?"

Another student teacher realized the serious responsibility she had for the safety of her young students as she wrote to her supervisor:

> Today, one of my kindergartners didn't come into the classroom after recess because he was writing with crayons on the outside table. It was hard not to wring his neck, but at least he wasn't hurt. I told him I was really scared when I realized he didn't come in with the bell. I cannot trust him anymore so will take him by the hand when the bell rings for the next few days . . . and I told him so. There's SO much responsibility!! Who knows what theory that is, if any! I did the best I could though with this child and will try to learn from my mistakes.

Toward the end of their student teaching assignments, most of the preservice teachers reflect about their overall experiences. This broad reflection is not required, but it is something that nearly everyone does. Formerly expressed feelings of discouragement appear to have dissipated as confidence has grown. Several of the student teachers have commented that their professors' supportive e-journal responses have helped them during difficult times. Two students' messages illustrate this kind of summative reflection. The first student commented, "I learned so much in this first teaching assignment!! And one thing I learned is that I will be constantly LEARNING. There is no end to the new information that becomes available to teachers . . . things are constantly changing!! That is what is attractive about teaching . . . constant changes for the betterment of our children and society."

The other student's comment is also typical of the end of student teaching:

> This has been an exciting, exhausting, uplifting, disheartening, enlightening, and baffling seven weeks. Think how much we've learned and experienced! I'm almost worried that my next student teaching placement may not be as challenging. Notice, I said, "almost." I am looking forward to the change I will have to make in handling the younger children I will be working with. I was told that my new school has quite a diversity of children from different backgrounds. That will be interesting.

Responding to E-Journals

As Keith mentioned previously, responding to e-journals takes time, but no more time (and perhaps even less!) than when responses are handwritten on paper journals. MaryEllen believes it is important to respond to e-journals in a timely manner, as close to the day of the original message as possible. Samples of some of her e-journal responses to student teachers' reflections include the following:

> Thanks for your great message! I'm so glad you're risking by trying some new things . . . and, of course, I'm delighted that your teacher is accepting your

ideas. That's what is so great about student teaching—there's lots of give-and-take. At any rate, you're terrific and your kids are showing such growth. Please take some time to feel really proud of yourself!

It's Tuesday night and I just read your great, reflective message. Now I understand all that you were talking about today when we conferenced. One thing to remember is that the type of reflection you're doing, while perhaps not much fun to do because it's a bit painful to admit some things, is a great way to keep on improving—because you tend to remember the things when you're teaching that you've thought about later after a lesson. Hang in there. Thanks for getting on-line and sharing your thoughts.

Hi! I'm glad you're feeling a bit better, and I'm sorry I didn't come forward with some of my concerns about your classroom situation earlier. The children don't seem to have a sense of appropriate behavior and it's difficult for you to come into that environment. Stick to your guns with them and remember that student teaching is a rare opportunity—you can try things out and see if they work . . . and then implement those which do. And, you're right. Teaching is not a popularity contest, and interestingly, the kids really do want structure and consistency. They know when their own classroom is out of control and remember most fondly those teachers who are firm but fair. I disagree with one thing you said. I think the children *will* really miss you when you're gone!

Occasionally, MaryEllen writes a group response to all student teachers about events or issues of common interest. Sometimes dialogues develop from these group responses. The degree to which a topic is continued or explored generally depends on how crucial it is and, of course, how much time responders have. An example of such a journal dialogue follows. The first message was written by MaryEllen to the entire group:

On Tuesday after seminar, I was thinking that you all seemed so tired that I'm not sure the discipline models made much sense to you. I'd encourage you to spend some quiet, reflective time reviewing each of the models. Even though they may not seem very grounded in reality, they really are and they can give you a foundation for decisions you make regarding how you plan your classroom discipline system. I'd love to know whether the models cause you to reflect upon what's happening in your classrooms now. Please let me know. Take care and nurture those kids!

Soon after her message was sent, she received the following e-mail from one of the student teachers:

I wanted to get back to you on the day of our discussion at seminar about discipline, but my life feels like a big blur whizzing by right now and I don't always get to everything I'd like to. Anyway, I knew that I needed to reflect on and digest the material that you presented in class. It's "sink-or-swim" with this discipline and classroom management stuff. Lots of what you said hit home to me. Just one example: Give the kids a sense of being heard and respected through active listening in order to diffuse tension. The same day you told that to us I had tried to sweep some problems under the rug instead of listening to a problem that the kids were having. I could read in their faces that they were not going to get anything out of any lesson that I would present until I had dealt with the problem. So, I stopped and dealt with it and it diffused the situation. Thanks for a great and much-needed lesson. I intend to go over my notes intently . . . but not tonight. I'm pooped.

MaryEllen then continued the dialogue with this individual student teacher and wrote back, "Thanks for your feedback on my suggestions. I'm glad they helped. Developing classroom management skills takes awhile (sometimes a LONG while!), so keep on keepin' on and don't be too hard on yourself if things don't always go perfectly."

What We Have Learned About Electronic Journals

Electronic journals reflect not the future but the present. Today's teachers must be able to access technological resources not only for their own use but for the use of their students. E-journals clearly promote reflection and present a powerful forum for introspection and discovery.

As alternative methods for preparing teachers are discussed, researched, and implemented, various technologies will play a large role in establishing new ways of stimulating thinking and reflection among new teachers. These same technologies are currently transforming teacher-education programs by providing effective distance learning opportunities, bringing together student teachers and new teachers for online discussions about common concerns and interests, and by offering experienced teachers as mentors who can continue the e-journal dialogues once new teachers have been hired.

We believe that electronic journals enrich the preparation of new teachers. The student reflections found in e-journals would be largely hidden from a professor in a traditional university course. Perhaps students might discuss some of their reflections and concerns with one another, but the chances of students being openly candid during office hours or in conversations are slim. The e-journal format, however, provides a protected environment—the student's home or in some cases, the computer lab—in which to write the personal reflections to the interested audiences of their professors and peers.

Thus, from our work in teacher-education courses and during student teaching, we believe e-journals have the following advantages:

- E-journals build a sense of community within a group of new teachers who are telecommunicating with each other and with the professor.

- University professors are able to respond to students' questions and concerns much more quickly, without a time lag that can limit support and assistance.
- The relationship between the professor and student is markedly changed by increased contacts and the personal nature of writing to each other on a frequent basis.
- Opportunities for group problem solving increase as both preservice teachers and their professor can read common e-mail concerns and share suggestions for dealing with an issue.
- Technology is demystified as preservice teachers become adept at telecommunicating and accessing educational resources.
- New teachers who have written in electronic journals are trained and ready to assume leadership in telecommunication in their schools and districts.

However, as with any innovation, we have a few areas of concern. These include the following:

- When the technology is not working correctly or the server is down or busy, preservice teachers become frustrated and often think it is a result of a failure on their part, thus increasing their anxiety about using technology.
- University equipment is often outdated or not working correctly.
- E-journals take time and commitment on everyone's part if participants are to respond to each other's writing in a timely manner.
- Some preservice teachers do not use e-journals for reflecting on their practice. Instead, they simply describe events in their day and problems they are having.[2]
- Some university professors and supervisors may not wish to have close relationships with students. E-journals do, indeed, bring students and professors together in a far more personal way.[3]

In all, we believe the advantages of electronic journals greatly outweigh the disadvantages, and that reflective, thoughtful, insightful teachers can help determine the course of education into the next century. Perhaps the following student teachers' e-journal excerpts say it best:

> I want to thank you for your special approach to student teaching through e-journals. With this approach, I was able to leave vital messages for you at any time of the day or night; and you were able to leave important messages for me regardless of whether or not I was home yet from class. When I needed help, you were there.

> There was always a way to communicate with all of the other student teachers in the same position as I was. With e-mail, we were able to share ideas,

helps, and information without getting a numb finger from constantly dialing the phone numbers of sixteen different people.

The diversity of on-line resources was helpful to me in planning and gathering information to use in my classroom. There were science and geology programs, and weather information which was helpful to my fifth graders as they were learning about weather during the Pilgrims' first winter in the New World. I was able to get information from university professors around the world and learn what students in other countries were studying.

In my opinion, electronic journals and telecommunication were invaluable to my student teaching experience, and I intend to continue to telecommunicate as a professional teacher. Thanks for opening the door for me.

Notes

1. For a fuller description of the TeacherNet project, see the Casey (1989) article listed in Works Cited.

2. This may be congruent with Valli's (1993) notion that reflectivity is not something that can be taught, only encouraged.

3. McIntyre & Tlusty (1993) suggest close relationships may be problematic for some professors.

Works Cited

Casey, J. 1989. "TeacherNet: Student Teachers Form a Community of Teachers." *California Technology Project Quarterly* 2 (1), 28–29, 68.

Casey, J., and Roth, R. 1992. "An Impact Analysis of Technology-Based Support in Student Teaching." *Teacher Education and Practice* 7 (2), 23–30.

Casey, J., and Vogt, M. E. 1994. "TeacherNet: The Wave of the Future. Towards a National Network of Educators." *Technology and Teacher Education Yearbook*. Charlottesville, VA: Association for the Advancement of Computing in Education (AACE), 677–79.

McIntyre, S., and Tlusty, R. 1993. *Electronic Dialogue Journaling and Its Effect on Reflective Practice with Pre-service Teachers.* A paper presented at the Annual Conference of the American Educational Research Association. Atlanta, GA.

Merseth, K. 1990. *Beginning Teachers and Computer Networks: A New Form of Induction Support.* Research Report 90–9. East Lansing, MI: The National Center for Research on Teacher Education.

Valli, L. 1993. "Reconsidering Technical and Reflective Concepts in Teacher Education." *Action in Teacher Education* 15 (2), 35–43.

Vogt, M. E., and Casey, J. 1994. *Promoting Reflectivity in Pre-service Teachers Through the Use of Telecommunication.* TeacherNet Project Report submitted to the California Technology Project.

For Additional Reading:

Alvermann, D. E. 1981. "The Possible Values of Dissonance in Student Teaching Experiences." *Journal of Teacher Education* 32 (3), 24–25.

Blanton, W., and Ulmer, C. 1996. *Dialogical Structures: Using Written Telecommunication to Create Productive Communities of Discourse in Teacher Education.* Paper presented at the annual meeting of the National Reading Conference. Charleston, SC.

Darling-Hammond, L. 1990. "Teachers and Teaching: Signs of a Changing Profession." *Handbook of Research on Teacher Education,* ed. W. R. Houston. 267–290. New York: Macmillan.

Darling-Hammond, L., Wise, A. E., and Klein, S. 1995. *A License to Teach: Building a Profession for 21st Century Schools.* Boulder, CO: Westview Press.

Pallante, J. 1993. "Selected Perspectives on Teacher Reform Efforts." *Action in Teacher Education* 15 (2), 25–31.

8

Writing Letters Instead of Journals in a Teacher-Education Course

Jane Danielewicz, Ph.D.

I tend to avoid rereading my writing because I find I'm embarrassed the second time around. That's why I love writing letters—I can send them away and never have to look at them again. But now I look back at the letters I got from Amy and those I sent to her, and I wish that I could have written to her all semester. She called me on every mistake I made in my logic, including my attitude problem, and her ideas were so different from what I think mine are.

Jessica

Writing letters as part of a course appeals to students because, like journals, they're relatively easy to produce. Letters are personal and expressive (first person "I" is a necessity), topics and issues are self-selected; the writing can be informal and stylistically relaxed. I ask students to write letters in an education course because it helps them engage with content material on their own terms, improves their writing, and creates community quickly—all necessary conditions for developing prospective teachers.

Besides the generic features I mentioned, students discover and value other qualities of letter writing. The excerpt above alludes to the pleasure of composing and sending letters (or, in Jessica's [1] case, of relinquishing them); the intense relationships that develop between correspondents (Jessica's wish to have written exclusively to Amy); the freedom to focus seriously on ideas and beliefs (Amy's critiques of Jessica's positions); and the opportunity to reflect and reconsider (Jessica's induced self-awareness). Letters prove to be a flexible medium for my students, who invent ways of using them toward their own ends, which is how I know the activity is a good one.

Why Letters?

Rhetorical Theory and Practice in the Teaching of Writing is a course devoted to introducing theory and methods related to teaching writing as a process. Students expect the class to improve their writing and develop their teaching abilities. Acting like writers and teachers during the course satisfies these goals. One way this happens is through the response and reaction letters students write weekly about assigned readings instead of keeping a traditional journal.

Why not a journal? Writing letters serves the same exploratory function as journals—students reflect on and articulate their positions relative to what they are reading—but with a twist. Changing the form from journal to letter significantly alters the writer's rhetorical aim by introducing a *real* audience. Journals are expressive writing directed toward the writer's self, whereas letters are transactional: Writers are obligated to communicate with readers. This difference has many ramifications.

But first some background: The course is required for undergraduate education majors who plan to teach English or language arts in either middle or high schools. Enrollment runs between fifteen and twenty; often it is the first education course students take. Currently, there is no associated field placement and the teaching practicum may be three to four semesters away. This isolation means that students must rely on their imaginations to envision the institutional contexts where they will eventually teach. The letter-writing exercise came about after an unsatisfying experiment with journals in which students wrote several pages a week in response to assigned readings. One semester the journals were minimal, perfunctory, and not representative of the strong positions my students advocated verbally. When I thought about it, only the entries we read aloud seemed memorable.

Sharing journals publicly did have the positive effects of bonding class members together and providing peer-generated models. But this practice made me uneasy since the journals were never intended to be public documents. To mediate this concern, I forewarned the class about reading aloud on each occasion. Compared to their usual entries, the ones they wrote for public consumption were longer and more thoughtful; this irregularity bothered me. Another issue was that some students were embarrassed to read aloud under any circumstances. Journals simply weren't working, but I hesitated abandoning them altogether. The personal reactions and interpretations they stimulated were critical to teacher development.

Doing Letters

The practice of reading journals aloud, however flawed, made it obvious that audience was a powerful, motivating force for student writers. The solution, I decided, was to assign a journal, but one that had an explicit external audience. The writing would remain involved and personal, but the conversations would be actual ones. What kind of hybrid was possible? Letters—rhetorical first cousins to journals—seemed promising.

At first I considered asking students to write me weekly letters that I would reply to by drafting a communal response. But such tight turn-around constraints discouraged me; furthermore, I already had too much authority and had no wish to be the ultimate audience. I decided instead that everyone (including the teacher) should write and receive weekly letters. (The resulting assignment is reproduced in the Appendix.)

The letter-exchange for a class meeting twice a week works in the following way. At the semester's start, each student is paired with a writing partner (either another student or the teacher) for the following week. In the first letter, writers respond to assigned readings or address issues raised in class discussion. These letters are delivered to respective partners during the first weekly class meeting. In response, each person then writes a second letter directly addressing the issues raised by their writing partner. This reply is traded in the subsequent class meeting. Since writing partners change weekly, any one pair writes and receives two letters per week. Students are asked to keep copies of all their letters plus save the originals they receive. Furthermore, they are required to be responsible writing partners. Class lists with phone numbers and e-mail addresses are circulated the first week. If students miss class, they must contact their partner and make arrangements to deliver the letter before the subsequent class or as soon as possible.

Partner assignment can occur informally, week to week, on an ad hoc basis. Sometimes in small classes during the final minutes, I simply ask students to pair up. If a student is absent, I will assign myself as his or her partner and contact that student by phone. Each student keeps a list of partners and doesn't repeat a pairing until there are no new combinations. Alternately, partners can be planned for in advance, which is the method I recommend for larger classes (over twenty students). Numbers are assigned to each student and the teacher, which then can be used to make a grid of weekly combinations for the semester. This arrangement helps students track their partners when they miss class and eliminates the need for the teacher to contact absent students.

At the semester's end, students review their abundant letter collections, consisting of about twenty to twenty-four letters they have authored and a similar number they have received. After rereading their collections (the process Jessica alludes to in the opening excerpt), they write a final letter to me as the instructor, in which they evaluate their collections as a *text,* making some generalizations about their development as writers and teachers. This ultimate letter and the accompanying collection constitute the final exam.

The final collections are graded on a pass/fail basis because I wish to reward student participation. I concentrate on reading and judging their summary letter, referring to the collection when necessary. A passing grade is awarded to students whose final letters draw on their collections to develop themes about themselves as teachers and writers, and who have written the required number of letters. In assigning grades for the course, I rely on other assessments, mainly their final project (a unit they have designed for teaching writing). If pass/fail evaluation is not appealing, individual instructors can weight the letter assignment more heavily by inventing an alternative grading system.

Letters as Journals

In the context of my class, it's the nature of audience that distinguishes letters from journals. In other circumstances there are, of course, many other differences between these forms. Why would audience make such a difference? Every text reflects the writer's consideration of several interacting elements: the author's purpose or aim, the audience, the social situation, and the genre or form. Of these, audience is the most difficult and elusive for student writers to really experience in artificial contexts like the classroom. However, audience also has the most potential to provoke powerful discourse because writers strive to reach readers who will be affected, changed, or moved by the writing itself. In fact, this theory was born out almost immediately in practice the first semester of letter writing although it was impossible for me to know at the time.

Not being privy to the exchanges between students, I had to discover the deeper effects in retrospect as I read the final collections. It turned out that responding was as important as writing the initial letter because students alternated between being writers and readers. Playing reciprocal roles increased what students learned and how they wrote. They were obligated by their expectant partners to read the assigned materials closely and to consider their readers' thinking patterns and preferences. Writing letters also changed social dynamics. Classroom relationships multiplied and deepened, while the power structures between teacher and students were somewhat realigned. Letter writing—done wholesale with predominantly student exchanges—diluted the teacher's authority but simultaneously strengthened peer relationships. An additional and surprising effect was that writing letters enlarged the discursive boundaries of the classroom. They created another space for dialogue alongside of and in between typical language events like whole-group discussions.

Reading to Write

Asking students to write journals can be risky business. Although I can usually count on some students having well-established habits of journal keeping and a positive attitude, others view journals as a deadly chore, an added responsibility, or an inappropriate demand to reveal personal information. These issues aside, a few students invariably report feeling unable to write in their journals especially when they encounter challenging reading assignments. "What's the point of writing," they complain, "about something we don't understand?" Although writing about a confusing issue often brings clarification, many students have never experienced this phenomenon. Still others fail to see any purpose whatsoever in writing a journal for themselves.

Writing letters takes care of several of these issues. A writing partner initiates a relationship with social responsibilities. Instead of writing for a grade, students write to fulfill their partner's expectations, which is authentic motivation for writing. Once committed, students feel compelled to read and think about the assigned readings in order to have something to write about, as Anne's letter suggests.

> Students still hate revising. I can totally relate because I know when I was in high school I hated it. It was pointless. I think of revising like exercising: you know that you should do it so you can look better, but getting motivated is one of the hardest things. You just wish you were born with the perfect body that doesn't need work, or you wish that your papers were always perfect. However after you exercise, or revise, you notice the results. I like the suggestions that *Community of Writers* gives for making revising more effective and less tedious. If students have the chance to write for real audiences rather than themselves, better papers will be written and students will want to revise.
>
> Anne

In her letter, Anne unconsciously refers to the process in which she engages, "the chance to write for real audiences," which not only reinforces but also translates into concrete action the ideas she's learning.

Because they are education majors, students are drawn to topics related to their development as teachers. Here Holly refers to a chapter about theories of group dynamics and the idea that *off-task* behavior (or "maintenance activities") may help individuals bond together and function collectively. Commenting on this new knowledge leads her to be self-reflective and analytical about her beliefs as a future teacher.

> Zemelman and Daniels' proposition that maintenance activities are less than evil took me rather by surprise. Perhaps because I was often frustrated in high school by teachers who wasted incredible amounts of time to initiate daily activities, I imagined that my classes would be like experiencing a whirlwind. From the second the bell would ring, I pictured myself spinning through material and activities, maintaining control over my students primarily by bombarding them with my own energy, expectations, and plans. That would explain why I fear becoming drained by and even disillusioned with teaching, though I have not yet entered my own classroom. I am beginning to realize that teaching requires the ability to continually improvise; I must allow my

plans to flow through the channels students open with their questions and comments rather than forcing discussions in directions I anticipate or for which I plan.

Holly

Not only does Holly confront her fears about teaching, but she also identifies a quality of effective teachers, "the ability to continually improvise." Further, she reorients herself vis-à-vis her imagined students, establishing her identity as student-centered rather than teacher-centered. Holly learns these philosophical positions not because I have taught them but through the act of writing her letter.

Writing for a Live Audience

Writing letters instructs students about the role of audience more efficiently than other methods I've tried. One difficulty with journals in school settings is that audience is either ill-defined, nonexistent, or artificial. Although it's a recommended practice, I've not had much luck advising students to *imagine* their audience. Instructors (myself included) who tackle this issue and attempt to clarify audience frequently end up portraying a hybrid or mixed reader. Who is the audience for assigned journals? The writers themselves, the professor, their peers, or a combination? How do students sort out these possibilities?

No matter how much I reminded students to think of themselves as an audience for journals, many inevitably wrote to me as the teacher. I was, after all, counting journals as part of their grade. But writing a letter to a single person cuts through the audience dilemma and disentangles the grading issue. Once the audience is identified, the writing task becomes easier, and students are quick to appreciate any adaptation that reduces the difficulty of writing.

While narrowing the audience to an individual (a peer or the teacher) doesn't solve all problems, it does make audience considerably more concrete. The writer must still decide how to address the reader (notice David's choices below), but at least the reader is a known entity. This contributes to more grounded and specific writing, and it partly eliminates vague or generic language.

Before I close, I would like to describe an experience I had this past weekend with a Medieval English teacher from NY state. I had studied very briefly *The Canterbury Tales* in high school but never fully enjoyed them. This professor read to me for hours excerpts from Chaucer's collections in very distinct Middle English Language. After reading each excerpt, he would go back and show me how the actual text is like music. I know, Debbie, this sounds boring as hell. My point is that this inspired me in ways that I had not been touched for a long time.

David

Writing to a real audience teaches important lessons about how audience shapes language. The experience of having to *write* and to *receive* a letter foregrounds the role of a good audience—a reader who relishes the text, who reads for meaning, who laughs at the jokes, and who takes the writer seriously. In the next example, it's the reader-writer relationship that energizes the language.

> Wow! I have the coolest thing to tell you. Actually, I'm sure you won't find it that fascinating, but I think it is awesome. Yesterday afternoon I was reading our assignment but my mind kept focusing on a friendship. So reading about freewriting, I was struck by the idea that I should write down all of the thoughts playing around inside my head and then share my writing with my friend.

> I want my students to develop the ability to truly freewrite—to express themselves in a stream-of-consciousness—and I want them to feel, just once, the powerful force of that stream crashing out of them and over them and onto the paper—forming meandering creeks of thoughts and feelings they perhaps otherwise would have never known they had. To me, the potential of such epiphanies of one's self make freewriting the most powerful resource and ability of any author.

> Holly

Because letters are a highly valued yet commonplace genre in the culture at large, most students have mastered their generic features outside of academic venues. Letter conventions are well-known; students need not struggle with questions of form. In contrast, other genres like the argumentative essay appear to be mysterious concoctions. Students expend a lot of energy figuring out and reproducing the seemingly arcane and depersonalized properties of academic discourse. The less exotic letter, much easier to compose, frees the writer up to think about content rather than form.

In an era when most composition programs include peer writing groups, these letters presented the first opportunity in college for students to read each other's writing for reasons other than to criticize or evaluate it. Teacher and students alike read the letters, not as critics, but as privileged recipients.

> Whoa—my hands are cold, not moving in rhythm. Sometimes I pretend I'm playing the piano when I type. I've always wanted the ability to express myself in creating sound. Words on a page are silent sounds, heard only in the mind of the reader. Listen.

> Mona

By the second or third round of letter writing, students had become an appreciative, understanding, and dialogic audience. Exchanging letters taught them that readers play many roles and, even more astonishing, that writing for readers who are not critics can be pleasurable.

Varying the audience—mostly writing to peers, occasionally to the teacher—heightened students' awareness of audience. Because of class size, each student was paired only once with the teacher. Not surprisingly, students are immediately self-conscious about writing to the teacher versus a classmate. Shifting the audience among individuals with different degrees of power revealed how such dynamics operate in the classroom. Also, students learned something about their own attitudes toward authority figures. Some who wrote freely and easily to peers found it troublesome shifting to teacher as reader (not as judge). They were in the groove when writing essays for the teacher, but the idea of writing a letter unsettled them. The letter forced them to analyze the distinction of writing *to* the teacher instead of *for* the teacher. Other students requested me as a writing partner, asking for outright approval and validation in their letters. One or two wrote their letter to me as if it were an academic essay. All of these effects were interesting and important—and ones that would never have occurred if students had been writing solely to each other or only to the teacher.

Epistolary Relations

Social relationships are what motivate good writing, but classroom norms can sometimes interfere with developing strong interactional dynamics. It's possible for students to meet in class three to four hours a week for several months yet rarely speak to each another. Weekly letters have the potential to transform a randomly assembled class of students into a functioning community, a process revealed in Mona's letter:

> How grand that we are partners this week! In our four classes together I have been able to watch you interact with other students, observing your mannerisms, expressions, and style of communicating. Now I will have the pleasure of knowing you through your writing—I am anxious to receive your letter!

Responding to the weekly letters insured the dialogue necessary to promote community in the classroom. The letters allowed students to become invested in each other. Acting like teachers, they generously offered suggestions or interpretations, gave advice, or reacted to new ideas or techniques just as Holly does here:

> The first thing I noticed about the student papers was that the majority of Ms. L.'s students write in black English vernacular. People *do* write the way they speak, and so clearly the language a student uses every day not only infiltrates, but essentially molds, her writing. What I found most interesting was the way in which Ms. L. responded to her students' use of black English.

While she does correct some errors, like repeated nonverb form disagreement involving the same verb (I be, we be, they is), she does not, by any means, attempt to alter every aspect of her students' writing to correspond with the conventions of standard written English.

Holly

Her partner, David, replies:

In your letter on Tuesday, you asked how are we supposed to analyze and grade written assignments in such forms as Black English Vernacular. In my English grammar class we studied BEV and how it does have distinct and solid structural rules. Although many of the usages may sound odd to us, there are grammatical patterns in every spoken and written sentence. My concern is with my students' well-being. I do not want to rigidly grade them on their slightly different dialectal usages or try to correct patterns that have been a part of their life from the beginning. Where my worries come flooding in is at my second goal: the preparations of my students' futures. By allowing dialectal differences in students' writing, am I hurting them for not learning English grammar as it is formally accepted?

David

Although they achieve no final solutions, the students articulated and shared their concerns, legitimizing them. Writing about language variation developed tolerance, understanding, and facilitation, important qualities for prospective teachers. These effects spilled over into the classroom. When dialect and writing style emerged as a discussion topic, Holly and David were able to offer thoughtful information and advice.

Writing partnerships between peers are more egalitarian than those between teacher and student. No matter how much a teacher decenters authority or relies on cooperative learning, teachers know more and have wider experience than students, which translates into greater power. But privileging peer interactions challenges traditional teacher authority. In this sense, letter writing poses low academic risk but carries high social value. Although it doesn't eliminate or negate the status differential between students and teacher, writing mainly to peers counteracts the power imbalance. Students understand automatically that peer-peer relationships are valued because the course structure deliberately fosters them. The chance for intensified peer contact is well-appreciated.

This method of communicating through letters has really been one of the highlights of the class. It has given all of us a way to discuss informally the ideas and suggestions that Dr. D. has tried to convey to us in the class. It is here that we gather every week and share our opinions, ask questions, and give help to our partner. I cannot speak for the whole class, but I have found them to be a source through which I got to know my classmates better.

David

As a correspondent, I am more like my students than at any other time during the course. Being a teacher—and a mentor, evaluator, grader, and authority-figure—means I can never be one of them, but writing and receiving letters allows me to bracket some of these roles. I can read (and reply) as myself.

Do you, as an experienced teacher, think that research papers are important or could I-Search papers take their place? I sort of go back and forth on this question. As I said before, I hated gathering information on Edgar Allan Poe. However, I am not sure that I could write an I-Search paper without having "gotten my feet wet" on a research paper. Macrorie seems to think that I-Search papers are much more important than research papers. I don't know what to think.

Linda

The issue of becoming a teacher was a dominant theme in the class letters. The following excerpt is my response to another student's negative reaction and sudden doubt about teaching after a day's observation in a public school. The medium of the letter permitted me to address her immediate concerns: the essay assignment and her conflicted feelings about teacher identity.

You might be reacting to the difficult task of keeping a wide-range of diverse students working productively all day. The class you observed is typically, not unusually, diverse. Sure, there is an extreme case—the child with Tourette's syndrome—but no class is without challenges among the students. Also the teacher you watched is still learning so of course she is not going to be perfect. She's doing many things right. So if it's not the kids per se or the teacher who was causing all the chaos, what was? I can't say for sure since I'm going on your first-hand report, but we could consider the goals the teacher sets for students in relation to her philosophy, and look at the range of activities over time—not just a day.
    Where does this leave you in terms of writing your philosophy paper? You are split between two poles—ideology, what you believe; and reality, what you observed in the classroom. I am suggesting that you stay on the side of "your beliefs" for now. Should you just forget about the reality out there? No—not forever, but maybe for the next week or so. The reality you saw was somebody else's classroom—not yours. It is one reality, but not the only one.

Jane

In letters, there are no false pretenses. I am spared the awkward position of having to deny being the teacher, yet I'm free to reveal other sides of myself. Sharing my intellectual life in personal ways not only improves my connections with students but makes the class alive and interesting.

Writing Another Dimension

Writing letters substantially altered and enlarged the discourse space of my classroom, an entirely unanticipated effect. Usually students participate through class discussions and small-group exercises, by writing papers or completing projects. However, writing letters constituted a wholly new dimension that students controlled, a site of interaction that had never existed before. In this extra dimension, conversations occurred between students, not aloud but in writing, and not during the class meetings but on account of them. Although the letters were institutionalized as a course requirement, these conversations escaped public surveillance. No one person was privileged to hear, witness, observe, receive, or respond to them all. But they were not entirely private either. Partial glimpses, tantalizing fragments, verbal references to the letters occurred constantly. In ways both mysterious and exciting, however, the letters remained an autonomous, distinct, and vital extra dimension. Students used this unclaimed space in many ways, often to raise idiosyncratic concerns or problems not addressed by the course. For example, in his letter David introduces the compelling, even unspeakable issue of racism, critical knowledge for teachers but not a topic included in my syllabus about teaching writing.

> Although we studied language as development this week, I wanted to write about race relations and multi-culturalism. What provoked me to think deeper about it was the waning hours of the O. J. Simpson case. By the time the case was over, the issue of race had drawn distinct boundaries between those who believed one way or the other. No matter how idealistic we are as future teachers, there no doubt will come a time when we will face situations such as "hate crimes," extreme prejudice from all sides, a differing opinion on the "right" curriculum to teach, and how politically correct we should be.
>
> I see so much segregation on this campus. This "imaginary racial wall" does not begin at Carolina, but is a microcosm of what the students have been brought up to believe and have experienced in the past. Sometimes racial boundaries are formed not by deep-rooted prejudice, but by the sheer ignorance of not knowing or understanding where the actual human being is coming from.

The letters encouraged students to shape the direction of the course by providing time and space to pursue whatever they wished. Because this extra discourse dimension exists outside the teacher's control, by default students were drawn into constructing the curriculum.

Reasons to Write Letters

Asking students to write letters instead of journals puts *real* writing—writing about content issues in order to connect with readers—at the center of the course. Letters encouraged my students to write regularly, with pleasure and devotion. On letter-exchange days, there was always a rush of anticipation, then silence as everyone read. Letters were written and delivered with care; they appeared decorated, in fancy typescripts, inscribed on textured or colored papers, punctuated by drawings. Students put more far more energy into the letters than the assignment required, a sign of their intrinsic value.

Using letters in lieu of traditional journals helps students learn information relevant to teaching English and engages them in the process of becoming teachers. Even though they're required, letters can still be acts of discovery and authentic communication. Since their content is open-ended, the letters accomplish whatever identity work is at hand for each prospective teacher. They serve as an outlet for students to express their commitments to teaching and as affirmations of their future selves.

One more reason. Assigning letters makes me a better teacher. I value the individualization that letters permit, especially to counterbalance the method of whole-group instruction predominant in college classrooms. Letters to an invested audience can transform a heterogeneous group of strangers into an engaged community of readers and writers. But most intriguing to me is how the letters create more space for dialogue, adding an extracurricular dimension to the classroom. Letters enable teacher and students alike to learn about teaching writing, to build serious relationships around intellectual issues, and to write many, many pages, almost without noticing.

Notes

1. All student names are pseudonyms. The letters have been edited and condensed for brevity's sake. I wish to thank the students who generously gave me permission to quote from their letter collections.

References

Macrorie, K. 1988. *The I-Search Paper.* Portsmouth, NH: Boynton/Cook Publishers.

Zemelman, S. and H. Daniels. 1988. *A Community of Writers: Teaching Writing in the Junior and Senior High School.* Portsmouth, NH: Boynton/Cook Publishers.

Appendix: Letter-Writing Assignment

*Course Title: Rhetorical Theory and Practice
in the Teaching of Writing*

*Response and Reaction Letters—due every Tuesday,
reply due every Thursday*

Description: Each week (for twelve weeks of the semester) you will write two letters to someone in the class in response to the assigned readings or to practices and events that occur in class. These letters should range from one to two pages. In the first letter of each week, you should react to or comment about the assigned readings. In addition, you may wish to discuss class events or develop an issue that is personally relevant.

     The first letter of the week is exchanged on Tuesday. After reading your partner's letter, write a letter in reply that addresses the particular concerns or issues raised. The second response letter is exchanged on Thursday.

Prompts: In writing your letters, you may find the following prompts helpful. You are not required to use the prompts, only if you so choose.

- What was most interesting about the reading this week? Why?
- What questions do you have about what we read this week?
- What prior experiences connect to the readings this week?
- What important points, issues, or practices were raised in class recently?
- Are there any interesting connections you can draw between the concepts or practices we read about this week compared with past weeks? Between this course and other courses?
- What reactions do you have to the tone, content, or advice given in the readings?
- What would you like to know more about?
- What was the most useful or captivating part of the readings?
- What critiques do you have for the advice, content, or methods advocated in the readings or in class discussion?
- How is what we're reading or discussing either helpful or irrelevant to your life as a teacher? Or to your life as a writer?
- What important issues are not being addressed by the readings?

Purpose: These letters serve the same function as a journal. You will be writing about your personal reactions or articulating your beliefs about issues and practices related to teaching writing. However, in other ways, these letters are quite distinct from a traditional journal. First, you are writing each letter to a specific audience and that audience shifts from week to week. Second, someone will be reading your writing in order to write a response. Writing and receiving letters will insure that all voices are heard, as well as enhance the classroom community. In addition, since each writer determines the content of weekly letters, you can highlight and explore your individual concerns as a prospective teacher of writing.

Writing Partners: Each week you will be assigned a different writing partner, another student or the teacher. Since I am a class member as well as a writing teacher, I will join you in the letter writing. Partners will write and exchange two letters per week. Remember, your partner is counting on receiving your letter. If you miss class, you must make every effort to exchange letters with your partner before the next class meeting or as soon as possible. Late letters are better than none at all! Consult the class directory of phone numbers and e-mail addresses.

Mechanics: Exchange your first letter of the week in class on Tuesday. After receiving your partner's letter, write a response and bring it to class on Thursday. You must keep a *copy* of all the letters you write. Also keep all the original letters you receive. Typed letters are preferable, but handwriting is permitted as long as the copies are legible.

Letter Collections and Final Exam: By the end of the semester you will have a large letter collection (20–24 letters you have written, plus the same number you have received). You will submit this collection, accompanied by a final letter addressed to me. Your final letter should be a reflective overview of your collection in which you explore how it represents you as a student, a writer, and a teacher. This letter collection will constitute the final exam. More information on the exam will be provided later.

9

TechJournals
Electronic Journal Keeping for the Technical Writing Classroom
Gian S. Pagnucci, Ph.D.

Date: Fri, 4 Oct 1996 09:08:27 EDT
From: DONALD FTGZ@wisc.iup.edu
Subject: Donald's Project
To: LGPR@wisc.iup.edu
Cc: PAGNUCCI@wisc.iup.edu, FTGZ@wisc.iup.edu
October 4, 1996

Cynthia,

    I would like to take a minute and tell you a little about myself. I am an English Pre-law major. I am a senior at our fine University of Indiana. I like to watch sports on television, especially football. My favorite team is the Steelers. I also like to listen to alternative music. I would have to say my favorite bands right now are Rusted Root, Everclear, and Pearl Jam. I am from the small town of Youngsville, Pennsylvania. It's up north in Warren county.

    Now that you know a little about me Cynthia I would like to tell you a little about the project I am working on. As you probably know I am redesigning a resume guidebook. The reason I picked this project is to perfect my own resume. I know my resume right now is in bad shape. I thought with this project I will get some valuable tips on how I can make my resume the best. As you know it is a competitive world out there and you really need something special in order to get noticed. Through this project I hope I can find that uniqueness that will get me noticed. Thank you Cynthia for reading my letter. I hope you will consider what I have said and choose my project to work on in order to perfect your resume.

Thanks,

Donald

Donald's e-mail to Cynthia is how journals look in my technical writing class: practical, collaborative, friendly, and work-oriented. My student, Donald (all names and e-mail addresses are pseudonyms), chats for a few sentences, and then gets down to business. The journal entry helps him shape his idea, cast that project in the light of other readers, and invite some interaction. It's a simple entry, but one that also looks ahead to the memos and business letters this student will eventually have to write on the job. I decided to start my chapter with this journal entry because I wanted to show right away that journal writing can work in the technical writing classroom. Donald's entry is well written, useful, and audience focused. As a technical writing teacher, this sample e-mail is what I want out of a journal entry.

Teaching Technical Writing

I teach at Indiana University of Pennsylvania (IUP for short). I've taught technical writing for awhile now, and before that I worked as a technical writer documenting computer software packages. To me writing, particularly technical writing, is very serious work. Do a poor job explaining how to program a VCR, and people end up having flashing clocks in their living rooms. Mess up the directions for a bank's savings program, and someone's hard earned money disappears. Incorrectly document how to dispose of a toxic cleaning agent, and people get injured.

My class is for advanced students who know a lot about their majors and will do a lot of writing in their future careers: safety science majors, nursing students, computer scientists. Tech writing is a hard class with a lot of work. My students have to prepare a real written product for real users. They have to write accurately and effectively. They have to desktop publish what they do and put it up on the World Wide Web. I like to think it's a course that will help my students later in life. Often it is.

So when a friend first asked me if I used journals in my technical writing class, I thought, "Of course not." I had the same concerns about using journals that I imagine many technical writing teachers have. I was worried that journals weren't serious enough writing, that students wouldn't work very hard on them, that the journals would take too much time to grade, and that I had too many other things to cover. I figured journals were fine for my beginning writing classes, but not for an upper level technical writing course.

A Philosophy for Using Journals

I've done a lot of thinking since then, and my technical writing students have done a lot of journal writing. Today I view journals as a great place for:

- brainstorming
- rough drafts and trial runs
- developing a writer's sense of audience
- encouraging collaboration
- helping make writing seem less intimidating

As I slowly integrated journals into my technical writing classes, I designed my journal assignments with three goals in mind:

- Journals should be work oriented.
- Journals should be collaborative and audience centered.
- Journals should be electronic.

Now I know plenty of writing teachers who successfully use journals in their classes without aiming for any of these goals. I wouldn't, in fact, want to say that all journal writing should be conducted with my goals in mind. However, these three goals match some of my fundamental beliefs about what it means to do technical writing.

Technical writers are always working to deliver technical information to an audience very much in need of that information. Not only is there a lot of work, but most of it isn't too exciting. So when I considered adding journals to my classes, I didn't want to increase the writing workload without some direct benefits to the students. In fact, what I really wanted was a tool that would help my students do their writing better. I hoped journals would be a task that encouraged brainstorming, drafting, and revision.

Because technical writing is so heavily focused on real audiences, I also didn't want journal writing to be an activity that taught my students to write only for themselves or their teachers. I wanted, instead, for the journals to help my students improve their ability to write for other people. That's why I decided that any journals my students kept would need to be shared with their classmates.

Finally, I know from experience that in the workplace all writing gets done on computers. When you hand your boss a memo, it better be laser printed, spell checked, and easy to follow. And when a written product goes to a client, it needs to outshine the competition. I teach my students how to design effective page layouts, how to use word processors and desktop publishers, and how to put writing on the Internet. To me, good technical writing starts with knowing how to use writing technologies. So I cringed at the thought of spiral-bound stacks of handwritten scrawlings. Sure, I've got tons of old notebooks stuffed in the closet of my study, but these days I do almost all my writing at the computer and about half of that writing is on e-mail. When I planned out journal writing for my classes, I decided probably the best way to keep those journals would, in fact, be to use e-mail. I figured it was important for my students to be experts at using e-mail anyway, and I also hoped to save some trees. Even better, this would emphasize to my students the way most technical writers do their work, by using a computer. And so that's how the electronic journal, what I call a TechJournal, arrived in my classroom.

I hope by now that I've been fairly convincing about the merits of using journals in technical writing classes. It's my belief that journals can be work driven, collaborative, electronic, and a wonderful learning tool for students. I'll move, then, to showing some specific examples of the journal-writing assignments I use in my classes and the types of writing they elicit. By examining the journal entries of my students, other teachers may not only be encouraged to adopt this approach in their classrooms, but also to modify it for the needs and abilities of their own students. The TechJournals I'm writing about here are just the beginning.

Getting Started

Most of the work I have my students do in technical writing is project-based. I ask each student to identify a potential client who needs to have some writing done. The work is performed for free, and the projects are limited to about twenty pages. Students have carried out projects like writing handbooks for student organizations, designing guides to workplace safety, and creating instruction manuals for fitness training and computer programs.

The students usually work on projects for their departments or the places where they're employed. The project gives them knowledge about the topic and the needs of the readers. It also keeps the students focused on writing for someone who will actually use the manual, not just a teacher who will grade it.

I start the course by introducing these projects and showing samples from previous classes. Once students have a general idea of what they want to work on, I get them started keeping their TechJournals to help them with the writing process. I like to introduce the journals early so students learn to view them as an integral part of their technical writing work.

The initial electronic journal assignment I hand out looks like this:

TechJournals, Vol. I

At some point you may have been asked to keep a journal of your thoughts and ideas for a writing class. Or perhaps you have been asked to keep a reading journal where you recorded notes and impressions about material that was assigned in a class. Or maybe you have your own personal journal or diary where you jot down thoughts and insights and things that happen to you.

Even if you've never kept a journal, the basic concept is simple. A journal is primarily a place to work with ideas. That's how we will be using journals in this class, as a way to push our thinking. And while many journals are private, we'll be sharing this writing, so that you can bounce your ideas off other people. Thanks to e-mail, that's an easy thing to do. In fact, one of e-mail's most valuable traits is that it allows people to spread ideas around quickly and inexpensively. That's why so many companies use e-mail as a work tool. It's also how we'll use e-mail in this class, as a way to help you do your writing work. For instance, if you're having writer's block, you can send out an e-mail to some of the other class members asking for help to get your ideas going.

Later, as we get more advanced, we'll use distribution lists and maybe a notes conference to share our ideas. But for now I want you to use e-mail as your thinking tool. We'll begin this TechJournal writing very simply. The only real rule is to concentrate on ideas. There are no rights or wrongs here, as long as everyone is polite. And don't worry about spelling or grammar. In your journal these won't be graded, so just do the best you can. You will get full credit as long as you complete each TechJournal entry.

Here's how to get started:

1. From the list of class e-mail addresses, pick two people you don't know very well.

2. Send these people an e-mail. For the subject of the message, please put your first name and the word "project" (i.e., Kisha's project). Also be sure to send a copy of this e-mail to the instructor. (At the cc: prompt type pagnucci.)

3. Include a date at the beginning of your message.

4. Write a short statement explaining who you are, what you are majoring in, and what some of your interests are. Be friendly.

5. Then write another short statement telling the people about the project on which you are working.

6. Finally, ask the people to write back to you with their ideas about the project. Ask them to tell you what interests them about the project. Also ask them for at least three specific ideas of things you could write about for the project or include on your web page. Be sure to have them explain these ideas so that you can use them if you want to.

For any messages you receive (the number will vary), send back a response that includes the following:

•   The date you wrote the message.

•   A short statement explaining who you are, what you are majoring in, and what some of your interests are. Once again, please be friendly.

•   A statement that explains what you think of the person's project. Please be supportive. Describe, in some detail, three ideas you have for what they can do with the project, either in regard to their web page or their hard copy document.

• If you would like, you might write these people for help with your own project as well.

• Also be sure to send copies of these e-mails to the instructor. (Again, at the cc: prompt type pagnucci.)

Please save all your messages and responses so that you can keep an on-going record of your journal writing. As the semester goes along, we'll look back at these TechJournal entries from time to time to see how your writing is progressing.

Early Entries

The journal entry from Donald, with which I began this chapter, follows the general guidelines of my first assignment. Here's another example:

Date: Mon, 14 Oct 1996 13:03:43.86
From: JENNY WLST@wisc.iup.edu
Subject: Jenny's Project
To: OTVJ@wisc.iup.edu
Cc: PAGNUCCI@wisc.iup.edu, WLST@wisc.iup.edu

Hello Steve! How are you? My name is Jenny. I'm a Safety Science senoir here at IUP. I will complete my degree in the fall of 1997. I'm doing my project on a Chain Saw Safety Program for Allenwood's Saw Shop. I will be covering the safety precautions that need to be followed, OO PPE, and relev Standards. The program has the potential to be used by Allenwood's clients. Please, send me three ideas that may aid in doing my project.

Thank You!
Jenny

Both Jenny and Steve were safety science students. They shared some common terminology, like Jenny's reference to "Standards" which meant the Occupational Safety and Health Administration's Workplace Safety Standards. In her first journal entry, Jenny is working on her idea for the type of project she'll do. Jenny's project idea is still pretty vague, but she has focused in on some people who might need a safety manual, customers buying chain saws at a local store. Certainly it's not a project I would have thought of myself. It's outside my normal experience. However, rather than limiting my students to the projects I might dream up, I've instead created a class where Jenny can take her own knowledge of her major and start applying it to a situation she thinks is important. This not only makes the project and writing easier for Jenny, since she'll have plenty of background knowledge to draw upon, but it's exactly what she'll have to do in the future when her career requires her to do on-the-job technical writing. Beyond that, allowing Jenny to choose a project that utilizes her knowledge of the safety science field also validates all the time and energy she's put into her education so far. It shows respect for Jenny as a developing professional and probably even helps her to see how much she's actually learned from being a college student.

Jenny's journal entry is low-key and easy to write. I give the students credit for writing the entries and tell them they don't have to be overly concerned with grammar and spelling as long as they are clear. This freedom enables Jenny to use a friendly, casual style full of exclamation points. She even has a couple of minor errors, like her word "senoir." (Of course, this was partly because we hadn't yet learned how to use the e-mail spell checker.) Like Jenny, Donald also uses a congenial tone as he talks about his favorite rock bands and says that his résumé "is in bad shape." The journal exercises are intended to be for a student audience, and these relaxed comments show that the students really do understand this goal. The students are not adopting an overly serious and formal tone in the hopes of impressing a teacher. Instead, they are writing to their classmates to get a little help, just as they would be likely to do with a colleague at a workplace office.

One of the real benefits, in fact, of this approach to keeping a journal is how it emphasizes for my students the idea that writing doesn't have to be a solitary experience. Many of my students come into technical writing class thinking that writing is a hard, lonely battle. E-mail journals are valuable in my teaching because they ensure that my students do their work together. Because students write their journal entries as e-mail messages, those entries automatically get sent to at least one other student reader, someone who is likely to respond.

As the teacher, I also get the messages, keeping me aware of what my students are working on and how their projects are progressing. I often quickly scan my e-mail before class, and then I'm prepared to touch base with the students and can respond to their individual needs. I can also directly write them a reply in e-mail. However, I generally avoid inserting myself into the journal-writing process because I don't want the students to become intimidated and feel like they're being watched. A few comments in class let the students know I'm reading their entries. If I reply to every message they send, though, I run the risk that my students will freeze up with writer's block because they're petrified I'll jump in and correct every grammatical error they make. Writing supportive, noncritical comments to respond to student work can address this concern, but students generally view English teachers as correct usage guardians no matter how we act.

Accurate grammar usage is important, of course, but what I'm mainly after is for my students to believe they have some power over writing, to have confidence that they really do know how to use writing for effective communication. Unfortunately, many of them don't believe they control their writing when they begin my course. I can't always get them to believe they do even by the end of the course. But the journal entries help since they emphasize the communicative nature of writing.

In many ways there's not actually much need for me to reply to the journal entries or for the students to even know I'm reading them. The entries themselves elicit responses from real readers, and that's usually all that's needed to make them valuable enough for the students to continue the process:

Date: Mon, 14 Oct 1996 13:57:21.26
From: STEVE BMGH@wisc.iup.edu
Subject: re: Cynthia's project
To: UGHT@wisc.iup.edu
Cc: PAGNUCCI@wisc.iup.edu, BMGH@wisc.iup.edu

Hi Cynthia,

This is Steve responding to your project proposal. Even though I am a Safety Major, I feel that we could help each other out in this project because my project is the same as yours—I'm making a handbook for the Safety Department. Some things you may want to include in your handbook or webpage: 1. History of the organization or department, 2. Essential info concerning Anthropology, like course curriculum, internships, co-ops, registration, etc. 3. On the web page, you may want to use links so that people may be able to find jobs. (Ex. JOBLINK) 4. Maybe you could add some helpful hints, such as learning to become computer literate, learning to use faculty office hours, or just getting involved with different organizations on campus. Finally, I think we should get together so that we can discuss how to make the actual handbook. That's about it, I will see you in class shortly.

Steve

Not all the replies are as good as Steve's, but when students see how useful the journal entries can be, it certainly encourages them to continue the work. Entries like Steve's also clearly show the kind of brainstorming that I believe journals are especially good at facilitating. In just a few short lines, Steve is able to help both himself and Cynthia move forward on their projects.

Of course, a class discussion might have achieved the same result, but this time there is a permanent record available for the students to consult. As a teacher, this feature of the electronic journal writing is especially helpful. When my students review each others' writing orally in class, I rarely can get them to take any notes about the discussions, no matter how many times I suggest it. I'm sure there are some students out there who actually like to take notes, but I don't seem to get a lot of them. What I do get, however, are students who love to receive e-mail and normally don't get much of it. By taking advantage of a technology my students already enjoy, my TechJournal assignments have a built-in advantage. Most teachers will take any advantage they can get to promote student learning.

Finally, many of the teachers I know who use journals in their classes say
they do so because journals encourage students to get lots of practice writing.
If practice is the goal, then e-mail accomplishes the same thing, and most students actually think it's fun.

Work in Progress

As the semester moves along, I encourage students to make active use of their
TechJournals to record their progress, share drafts, and look for help. To emphasize that the journal writing is directly related to the work they're doing, I
give my students the following assignment a couple of weeks into the semester:

TechJournals, Vol. II

As you'll recall, I got you started on these TechJournals by sharing a few ideas
about your project proposals. I would like you to continue the journals as a
way to further share ideas and to get help with any writing difficulties that
come up as you are creating your projects.

   In your role as a project manager, I would like you to make one
TechJournal entry each week to provide me and your project advisor(s) with
an update on your progress. This update should discuss the following:

- Previous project status—Where did you leave off?

- Current project status—What did you accomplish this week?

- Goals for the next week—What do you plan to do in the coming week?

- Instructions to project advisor(s)—What parts of the project would you
  like your advisor(s) to review?

- Difficulties you are having—What do you need help with?

- Successes you have had—What new things have you learned over the
  week about the web, your project, etc.?

- Ideas you have had—What new ideas and plans do you have for your
  project? As always, put things in a positive light. Remember, bosses prefer success.

   E-mail copies of each TechJournal entry to me (at: pagnucci) and to your
project advisor(s). In addition, you may want to cc: a copy to yourself.

   Also be sure to print a copy of each TechJournal entry so that you have
a record for your files. Even in the electronic age, companies want accountability.

On the Job

My second TechJournal assignment gives students a range of options about
which to write. The assignment also asks the students to send their TechJournal
entries to their project advisor(s). Each student in my technical writing course

serves as a project advisor for one or two (depending on the class size) of their classmates' projects. Project advisors edit and proof drafts and, more importantly, become an audience for the TechJournal entries. As the semester progresses, students often use their journals to ask their project advisors for specific kinds of help:

Date: Mon, 28 Oct 1996 20:42:34.17
From: DONALD FTGZ@wisc.iup.edu
Subject: response to your project
To: BMGH@wisc.iup.edu
Cc: PAGNUCCI@wisc.iup.edu, FTGZ@wisc.iup.edu

Steve,
    I am writing about your request for ideas about your project for technical writing. Safety science is out of my league, but I have worked at a mail order company and have had a lot of experience with their safety procedures. Maybe you should include in your handbook some statistics on graduates who get a safety science degree and land a good job. A lot of freshman change their major, because they do not know what job they can do with their chosen field of study. So they get scared and change it to something general. I think this would be an asset to your manual.

    Good luck, Donald

Date: Wed, 30 Oct 1996 13:41:03.08
From: STEVE BMGH@wisc.iup.edu
Subject: on Donald's ideas
To: FTGZ@wisc.iup.edu
Cc: PAGNUCCI@wisc.iup.edu, BMGH@wisc.iup.edu

Donald,
    Thanks for taking the time to reply to my e-mail. Your idea of including statistics on job placement rates for Safety Grads. is a great idea. This info. would be very supportive in my handbook.

    Thanks again, Steve

This exchange shows some of the great potential for these journals. One student taps into his personal experiences to help another student in a totally different field. Along with making prior knowledge accessible, the journals help students really think about who the audience for their writing is. When Donald suggests to Steve that the student handbook needs particular content to help freshmen who get scared about their majors, he is really helping Steve to envision an audience. It turns out this fear was not something Steve had considered, so in his reply to Donald, it's clear that Steve is now ready to make some revisions.

    The wonderful thing that happens here is that Donald not only convinces Steve to revise the handbook, he also suggests to Steve how to do that revising.

Steve is happy to get the advice. Donald, meanwhile, comes away realizing he actually knew how to help Steve with writing the project, which encourages Donald to have confidence when doing his own writing. Of course, I could have helped Steve revise his project during a teacher/student writing conference, assuming I was smart enough to think of the same idea Donald did. Instead, Steve has gotten the help he needed, and Donald has earned the praise. Both students have learned something valuable without a teacher getting in the way.

Along with making journal entries that give advice, students also constantly use their TechJournals to provide their project advisors with progress reports:

Date: Wed, 20 Nov 1996 15:56:34.62
From: JENNY WLST@wisc.iup.edu
Subject: Jenny's Project
To: OTVJ@wisc.iup.edu, RTNV@wisc.iup.edu
Cc: PAGNUCCI@wisc.iup.edu, WLST@wisc.iup.edu
Nov. 20, 1996

This is to let you know how my project is progressing. My web page is approximately half way done. Next week I plan to finish the web page and the draft of my project. Next week I will need you to read over my rough draft. My web page is currently at a stand still until I speak with the owner of the saw shop. I need to show him what I've accomplished and get some ideas on where to go next with the web page. As for my project I've photocopied some pictures to incorporate into the text to give somewhat of a visual aid. The layout for my project has been developed. Now all I need to do is sit down and type the text.

Jenny

The writing here is very practically oriented. Jenny is focusing on what she's done so far and what needs to be done next. She is approaching her project in stages, working on one piece at a time and looking ahead to the overall picture. The journal is helping her focus on the process of her work. The journal serves as a reminder of what work is most immediately pressing and emphasizes that the writing is ongoing rather than a paper to be started and finished the night before it is due. By sharing progress with their classmates, all students have a way to gauge how well their work is going. Reading each others' journal entries, students can easily decide whether they are ahead or behind. Instead of the teacher directing every move the students make, telling them exactly what to do and when, TechJournal sharing helps everyone stay motivated and on track. The journals can also help make other students aware of any parts of their own projects that they may have overlooked.

Additionally, like Donald and Steve's journals, Jenny's entry shows that she is thinking more and more about her audience. Jenny stops working on the web page so that she can consult with her readers to get help with her writing. I believe Jenny is honing her instinct for knowing when and where readers will get lost. As she identifies such problems, she decides to seek real response.

Jenny no longer views her writing in isolation. Instead, she is focused on the writer/reader relationship.

Finally, by concentrating on reporting their progress in regular TechJournal entries, students are also preparing for the type of constant accountability demanded at many companies. Writing journal entries helps my students get used to describing what they've accomplished. In my own experience, that's a skill bosses look for.

Wrapping Things Up

As the semester draws to a close and students come under the pressure of final exams and projects, their journal entries get pretty short, which seems reasonable to me. By then, hopefully, the journals have served their purpose. In fact, most of the final entries are filled with comments like "Everything's almost done" or "How will I ever get this finished?" or "Hey, I think this has turned out pretty darn good."

I considered finishing my chapter with one of these triumphant little messages. However, it is probably more effective to include the cover letter from one of my students' final projects. The things I hoped journal writing would do for my students were to foster their orientation toward work, encourage collaboration and their development of audience awareness, and promote their use of technology. The electronic journal entries already included should provide some evidence that the last two goals were achieved. But what about the first goal? Did the TechJournals help my students gain a better sense of how to write as professionals? Showing exact proof is difficult to do, but one final piece of quality student writing makes the case:

980 Maple St.
Indiana, PA 15701
Dec. 16th, 1996
IUP ASSE Student Section Advisor
Safety Sciences Department
Indiana, PA 15701

Dear ASSE Advisor,

I am pleased to submit my completed IUP ASSE Student Section Handbook and Internet Web Page. If you'll recall from our meeting, I decided to make a Student Section Handbook that would be available to all interested Safety Majors. My goal for the Handbook was to increase membership in our successful Organization by providing information on our meetings, benefits of membership, and scholarships. Also, I wanted to construct an interactive Web Page that would be accessible to anyone in the world. It would allow other Student Sections to see what we have to offer, as well as to keep in touch and share ideas. This Section Web page provides detailed information on our Committee work. I have enclosed a copy of the handbook, and you can access the Internet Site at http://www.iup.edu./~bmgh/. Both sections of the project will help raise awareness about ASSE simply because many passive or uninformed students will find out about it through word of mouth. As Advisor to the Section, I hope that you can provide me with some feedback about the accuracy of its contents and possible areas of expansion.

Working on the project itself went very smoothly. The Handbook had some organizational flaws initially, but your assistance proved very helpful with that pitfall. The Internet page had minor problems, like implementing graphics and lining up the document. However, it was fun and relatively easy because the Web Page contained much of the same information as the Handbook. Also, I did have difficulty contacting all of the ASSE Chapter Webmasters, but I will continue to contact them because I will have them provide a link to our Section.

The highlight of the project is that I have received e-mail from interested students. Since this project is already showing positive support, I would recommend maintaining a Webmaster and a Committee for the page in order to make additional changes or corrections. It would be a good idea to have a brainstorming session at each of our meetings so that members can suggest additions to the page. Finally, I hope that you can help increase faculty support because so many members are apathetic to our cause. In turn, their help will provide us with much needed support in the future. I would like to thank you for allowing me to work on this project. There is no doubt that it will help our ASSE Section remain as one of the elite in the country. It was a valuable experience for me because I have made a positive contribution to ASSE. I will stay in touch, and I hope that you find my project informative and useful.

Sincerely,
Steve Rogers

Clearly, this is a student who is developing a keen sense of how to write for other professionals in his field. Steve writes well, with a strong sense of who his audience is and what they need to know. He maintains an even, professional tone, completely appropriate for the task at hand. Did the journal writing advance him to this point? I believe so. Steve even mentions that getting feedback about the project, the kind he received from the TechJournal assignments, was what made his class work such a valuable experience. He's displaying exactly the kind of writing skills I hoped the journal keeping would promote.

I realize, of course, that the TechJournals were not the only things contributing to the success of Steve's final letter. I imagine his natural abilities, the other class activities he worked on, and the writing he had generated in prior courses all helped him create a strong letter. One specific class activity is never the secret key to learning. Instead, as teachers we have to give our students lots of tools and skills for approaching the work and challenges they'll face in the future. TechJournals are one such tool, so I'll keep asking students to write them.

10

Traditional or Electronic
Using Dialogue Journals for the First Time in Accounting Classes

Alan Rogers, M.B.A., C.P.A., and
Jerry VanOs, M.B.A., C.P.A., Ph.D.

From: Sammie Nichols
To: J-VanOs
Date: 9/5/96 6:32 pm
Subject: WEEKLY JOURNAL

This is my first e-mail message ever. Please let me know if it is received. I am a little tentative about this e-mail and internet assignments becouse [sic] it is something I am totally unfamiliar with. However, I am excited to learn how to use the internet and send e-mail before I am totally left in the dust. I have some familiarity with computers but not much involving computers and accouting [sic]. I am interested to learn the applications involved.

Although college students take English and writing classes, it is not uncommon for graduates who go into professional fields to feel their education was somewhat lacking in the area of writing. More precisely, writing skills that students supposedly learned in English were often never applied in courses in the major. We both recall having to write almost no papers in our college accounting courses. Consequently, asking students to write formal papers in the accounting classes we now teach creates a great deal of discomfort. For instance, how can we ask students to write formal papers when we doubt our expertise in correcting grammatical errors? The list of grammatical or sentence errors—subject-verb agreement; verb tense consistency; punctuation; sentence fragments or run-on sentences; choppy, awkward, or illogical sentences, etc.—loom endlessly to those of us who don't feel our English or writing background is strong. The higher rhetorical concerns of structure, unity, focus, coherence, conciseness, and sufficiency seem nearly impossible for an accounting teacher to critique. Incorporating writing into accounting classes, however, is the trend in accounting education (May 1989), and many accounting professors like us feel the pressure to do so.

Importance of Communication Skills in the Accounting Profession

Professional experience as CPAs in public accounting clearly taught us that the skill of compiling accounting information is very important. No matter which area of public or private accounting a professional is in, being able to communicate an issue in an understandable manner to a client is equally as important as having technical expertise. This skill—the ability to communicate the complexities of accounting issues in technical or nontechnical jargon—can separate the successful accountant from his or her counterparts.

Because of the nature of the business in public or private accounting, auditing, tax, systems, not-for-profit, or other areas, accountants find that much of their work needs to be documented in some type of written form. Documentation can be through a memo, report, or formal letter to a client, agency, coworkers or others. Knowing that clear and effective writing skills help students be competitive in the job market and successful in their careers, we wanted to help them connect their writing skills to their chosen major, accounting. This chapter, then, describes our separate use of journals and our combined reactions to using this form of writing in two accounting courses.

How Alan Got Started Using Journals

A workshop on journal writing was offered at Westminster College, and I (Alan) decided the seminar might help me incorporate more writing into my accounting courses. Initially, I joined the workshop to learn more about formal writing assignments that I would require of students and correct—despite my lack of background in and feelings of inadequacy about writing. I envisioned that requiring a formal paper might build on the writing skills students had learned in other courses and help them incorporate these skills into accounting classes. To my surprise I found the workshop seminar focused on doing the more informal, sustained process of journal writing as a means of including writing practice in any discipline. I found the reasons for using journals might fit well my goals for writing in accounting classes because journals

- foster the development of critical-thinking and problem-solving skills,
- give quiet students a chance to speak and allows a teacher to hear all the voices in the class,

- allow teachers to periodically check students' understanding of course material,
- provide teachers with windows into students' thinking and thinking processes,
- give students writing practice and a place to organize their thoughts,
- enable students to discover what they know and identify what they don't know,
- let students clarify their thoughts and focus on specific topics or issues,
- make all students active learners, and
- can improve teacher-student relationships.

I was intrigued with the possibilities of nonthreatening journal writing. Because journals are a kind of first draft type of writing, I didn't need to focus my attention on mechanical or spelling errors. Instead, I could use the writing as a quick check on students' understanding of concepts and topics I had covered in class. I could see the potential of having students write about what part of the topic was still confusing or difficult to understand. I could even see students using journals as a way to help organize the knowledge presented to them. Journals would also help promote writing fluency, and then I could use journals as preparation for more formal writing assignments.

A Traditional Dialogue Journal in Alan's Intermediate Accounting Class

To begin my experiment with journals, I decided to use just one section of Intermediate Accounting, a small class of only thirteen students. The small class gave me more flexibility and less pressure. I knew that integration of journals into a course is very important. The journal assignment needs to be done in a way that makes it appear to be a normal part of the class. Accounting students could be resistant to the inclusion of journal writing. Some of my students admitted majoring in accounting because they thought they could bypass classes that required writing. Thus, how the journal was initially described and set up in the class turned out to be extremely important.

I had invited two guest speakers to talk about the characteristics a graduate should possess to be successful in a professional career in accounting. Without any prodding from me, the two speakers emphasized the importance of good communication skills, both oral and written. One speaker commented on how his job continually involved summarizing or communicating accounting issues in written form. Following the two speakers, I showed a short movie—*Accounting: 360 Degrees of Opportunity*—that also emphasized the importance of written communication.

Even though I hadn't purposely set it up this way, the speakers and movie lent extra credibility to my wanting to incorporate more writing into the class.

I provided specific but basic guidance on the journal-writing assignment that included its purpose (see Appendix A). I especially emphasized that journal writing involves expressing thoughts in a person's own words, which in turn involves formulating and clarifying those thoughts. In this sense, writing is thinking. I told students to look at journals, then, as a place to practice thinking.

I kept the physical format of the journal quite open: It could be a loose-leaf notebook, a spiral or bound notebook, or a steno pad. Students could use pen, pencil, or word processor to create their entries. The only specific requirement was to leave enough room on the left margin (about two inches) for my responses.

I made sure students understood the style of writing expected. The informality of journal writing reduced my fear of trying to become an English teacher, and it also decreased the anxiety many accounting students experience when given the assignment of a formal paper. With *no* emphasis placed on grammar, punctuation, and spelling, the beginning objective in writing was on thinking, formulating thoughts, and organizing concepts.

Students also seemed to appreciate some guidance on the possible content of the entries. I left the choice of content quite open but discussed student-selected content, topics related to the course, and focused questions I would provide. Content discussion made this new process of journal writing less threatening to students. At the beginning, I suggested writing on one thing learned from a particular class, summarizing the main point of a lecture, describing one or more questions about the topic being discussed, or sharing a discovery made as a result of the class or reading. I also introduced possible topics I wanted students to address.

Another very important consideration for students was the audience for their journal entries. Their journal writing would be directed toward the reader (in this case me, the teacher) and would not be shared with other students unless permission was granted by the writer. Students also asked about expected length of entries, and together the students and I decided length would be in time, not words, paragraphs, or pages. Length of the content was not the issue; the issue was having accounting students get used to and buy into the process of writing in journals. Students were expected to spend between ten and fifteen minutes maximum at the beginning, a minimum of twice a week. Some writing would be done in class, and some would be out of class. Journals were due every two weeks, and my responses would be as a real reader, not as judge or critic.

Alan's Responding to Journal Entries

In the workshop I had experienced how critical the responses to journals are in keeping students' enthusiasm for writing their entries. Responding appropriately was a major concern for me, and initially I questioned whether I could do it effectively. My worries were typical of any teacher trying a new writing technique for the first time. Would I say the right thing? Would I unknowingly offend a student? How would I handle a truly bizarre entry?

In the workshop participants had discussed the kinds of responses students said were most effective and helpful. Those responses included comments that helped generate new thoughts, interacted with their ideas, and indicated some worth in the writing. Good instructor comments might include suggestions or questions that encouraged future research.

I was also concerned that responding meant writing lengthy comments that would be extremely time-consuming. I didn't want to get responding cramps and wondered about using specific, concise phrasing such as "well-stated" or "clear example." Would students find more terse comments useful also? I decided to try these, too, and use longer comments to answer questions students asked in their entries.

Abby, one of the more verbal students in the class, let me know early on how effective journal writing was for her and how much my comments meant. At the end of one of the first journal entries, she wrote:

> I think the journals are a great idea. I really miss writing and I know I could use the practice. It seems that writing is an important part of accounting. In class we heard about the importance of writing from both of the speakers and from the movie.
>
> The journals also seem worthwhile because from the comments you made on them. I could tell you must have spent a good deal of time reading the journals which means a lot. It gives me more of an incentive to put forth an effort on these.

Because of my own tentativeness about using journals in accounting classes, I was impressed by how quickly Abby bought into the new emphasis on writing, and I couldn't help writing an exuberant response to her:

> Because journals are a new concept for me, I have questioned whether to have students do one. Your two short paragraphs have convinced me differently. I'm psyched!! I hope I can get you as *enthusiastic* about accounting as you have made me feel about journal writing!! Thank you!! Thank you!!

The Electronic Journal in Jerry's Accounting Information Systems Course

The increase in the popularity of electronic messaging, or e-mail, to communicate in business has been tremendous in the last five years. Part of e-mail's popularity as a method of computer-mediated communication stems from its being so easy to learn. Because my Accounting Information Systems course deals with technology, I (Jerry) wanted accounting majors to use as many different electronic vehicles as they could during the term. I believe that using e-mail was the fundamental step to students moving on to other electronic applications. I also saw students creating an electronic journal as a way to improve communication between them and me and as a means for delivering the course curriculum. At the beginning of this chapter, Sammie's tentative "first e-mail message ever" demonstrates exactly why I chose to start with e-mail journals as the introduction for other technology. A bit fearful because of unfamiliarity, Sammie represents those students who are interested in technology, in communicating with teachers, and who want to learn practical applications. More than anything, e-mail journals are a good way to start so that students aren't "totally left in the dust" technologically, as Sammie points out.

I asked students to submit a weekly e-mail message on any topic of their choosing (see Appendix B). Some students were skeptical that any topic or length of message would be acceptable. I assured them the requirement was one message—any type, any length—per week, and Suzanne tested my openness right from the beginning: "Hi, there, I don't really have anything to say. This is my weekly e-mail." This barren entry was perfectly acceptable; I knew with practice student entries would improve in depth and content.

For the assignment I provided a firm deadline (the week's end at midnight) and a definite number of weekly entries. I told students all entries would be responded to by me, but only those entries that occurred during the week's time frame would be counted toward the required number. Students could write more frequently, but they could only record one per week toward their requirement. This setup ensured that students would write over time and on a more consistent basis, and that as the instructor, I wouldn't be overwhelmed at the end of the term with all the makeup e-mails. I allowed none of those, and students took me seriously as the following e-mail suggests:

From: Suzanne Lennox
To: J-VANOS
Date: 10/24/96 1:44 p.m.
Subject: Weekly E-Mail

Dear Jerry, These days I need all the points I can get and missing a weekly e-mail could mean the difference between a nervous breakdown and making it through one more week without having one—yet!! I think I missed the deadline for the e-mail.

My objectives for using an electronic journal in an accounting information systems course included the following:

• to improve written communication and develop an appreciation for communicating via an electronic platform,

• to address issues of concern or interest relative to course material,

• to communicate recommendations and suggestions to the instructor for further improvement of the course,

- to develop the ability to generate ideas and recommendations about accounting related topics, and
- to respond to material read or experienced in the course.

Students could either e-mail from home or work, or they were set up with accounts on our college network. One of the best features of the electronic journal assignment is that it provided a means for students to communicate with me outside the scheduled classroom and office hours. Many of the students in the class were nontraditional students with professional and family commitments that prevented them from discussing course material with me during regularly scheduled office hours. The electronic journal, then, provides a forum for one-on-one dialogue regardless of time or place.

Similar to the traditional journal, the electronic journal encourages students to ask questions or share concerns with the instructor. In a formal classroom environment, many students are inhibited from asking questions they perceive other students already know. E-mail journals allow students to ask the questions they did not ask in class or express their confusion and need for further help.

From: Becky Tomczek
To: Jerry VanOs
Date: 9/19/96 9:18 am
Subject: AIS—Electronic Assignment for the week of 9/16/96–9/20/96

After today's class, I am sure you will have a few messages regarding the complexity of the flow charts. Data processing cycles seem confusing to the newcomer, like myself. I understand the elements of a DFD or conceptual framework probably because it is limited to 4 symbols, but the physical flowcharts uses a diverse range of symbols. In regards to the homework questions reviewed in class, I was confused on the use of squares, rectangles, and circles; not necessarily why we use them, but how we use them. Guess you could say the entire assignment has been a challenge for me, which explains why I did not have much completed for class today. I understand the flow of data, just not the transformation process or how the data is stored or filed. I plan to reread the chapter, and practice with the homework before Thursday, but you never know—you may have another message from me before then.

Thank you for your last reply. It was helpful in many ways. See you Thursday!!!

Once I understood the problems students were having, I could either provide answers individually via e-mail, or I could use the problems or confusion in subsequent class sessions.

On personal questions or advisement needs, individual e-mail response seemed the best route. For example, Joe solicited my advice directly:

After reading the first chapter, I can see why everything I am reading these days claims that the future of accounting is in consulting. What I would like to know is how a guy gets into the field of information systems. Do I need a computer science degree or an information systems degree? I had planned on going into auditing for a few years and then trying to move into consulting— do you think that sounds like a smart idea, or is there a better way? The future is clearly in information systems and consulting, and I would like to be a part of this. Any guidance you could give me would be greatly appreciated.

An individual e-mail addressed his questions.

How Students Used Journals in the Accounting Courses

As teachers, both of us found almost no hesitation on the part of our accounting students to participate in the journal-writing process. Some students started slow, writing maybe a few lines or one paragraph, while others jumped on the idea, writing extensively and frequently. Students often began writing on anything that came to their minds, but even though it wasn't required, almost all made reference to something that related to course material. We found students used the journals in a variety of ways. Some of the more significant uses follow.

To Connect Unassigned or Additional Reading to Course Material

Stan used his weekly e-mail to tell Jerry about an article he'd read:

> I read an article in the Wall Street Journal last week about firms having problems with their AIS. The system was counting some accounts payable twice and failed to detect the mistake. It also failed to take advantage of trade discounts (2/10 n 30) for some of their payables. The article said that these problems were costing millions of dollars for various firms. It seems like it would be easy to include safeguards in the AIS that would protect against these potential problems. Do you think the person that created the AIS made a mistake or did the system fail?

To Express Frustration or Confusion

Part of Sammie's e-mail is simply letting off steam, a kind of catharsis:

> In trying to complete problem four on chapter 11, I became really disgusted with myself. I took the finance class in which I learned the concepts of NPV and IRR. I knew this stuff inside and out. And now I couldn't remember how to do it to save my life! It's disturbing how fast you can forget what you have

learned without using it. I'll be digging out the old finance book real soon! At least I have a reference.

To Write Themselves into Understanding

With the early success of the journal writing and the clear communication the entries provided, Alan tried using writing to help students work through difficult accounting concepts. In class he discussed the complex rules that govern gain and losses on exchanges of similar and dissimilar assets, including receiving and paying boot with the exchanges. Students often find this topic hard to grasp, and he saw his students were lost.

Spontaneously he decided to use a focused journal write and asked students to compose a memo to him explaining and summarizing the rules for recording exchanges of similar and dissimilar assets, including transactions that included the receiving and paying of boot. Students initially balked at his apparently absurd request. "How can I explain it to you? I don't understand myself!" a number of students blurted out almost simultaneously. Alan's response was to ask calmly for students to explain the concept in their journals.

When students came into the next class session, Alan was gratified to find the journal experience worked to help students discover what they knew, identify what they didn't know, and clarify and organize their thoughts. Students' understanding of the concept was factual and accurate, and most students commented that once they had to sit down, think, and explain it to someone in writing, they actually understood the concept and process. Students had discovered how their journal writing was an effective tool for learning, and Alan realized this informal memo writing in the nonthreatening form of a journal entry was only a few steps removed from a more formal memo assignment he would make later in the course. The journal writing, then, served as a bridge between clarifying ideas, drafting informally, and writing formally.

To Create Meaningful Dialogue with Their Teachers

Both of us found students' entries were, for the most part, enjoyable to read. It was clear to us right from the beginning how the dialogic nature of journals Jana Staton (1987) described over ten years ago helps develop one-on-one relationships with students. We found the formality of the professor/student relationship really disappeared and students chatted on paper or computer screen with us in a natural, conversational manner. We found students asking questions more on an individual basis than they would have done in a classroom setting. As Alan noted:

> Students would share with me what they didn't understand or questions they
> had about certain topics they didn't understand. A lot of the time the majority

of the students had the same concerns. The students were much more comfortable telling me in written form about the part of lectures or concepts that they didn't understand individually than they would in a classroom setting with other students. This gave me the opportunity to regroup and approach a topic a little bit differently the next day emphasizing those areas that students had concern about.

To Provide an Outlet for Humor and Creativity

Some people have the mistaken impression that accountants and, hence, students taking accounting majors are deadly serious people, but even we were surprised by students' use of their journals to make jokes or write creatively about the intricacies of accounting. One e-mail Jerry received began with "I can't believe you didn't wear a tie today in class! What kind of an example are you setting for us future accountants?"

In Alan's class Abby's explanation of exceptions was an especially enjoyable entry to read:

> My enthusiasm for tax accounting has considerably plummeted today. At first (before I attended class), I felt overwhelmed by the entire subject. It seemed that as soon as I understood the rule, there were many exceptions to the rule. Then, what made it even more confusing was that there were exceptions to the exceptions. It got pretty bad. I was actually waiting for a rule to come up that stated: "If your name is Helga, and your husband's name is Hans, then you get a deduction of $200. However, if Hans is an ex-convict from Cuba, then you would have to take his mother's adjusted gross income for 1985 and deduct the greater of the two totals." But, after class, I was a little relieved because I seemed to have gotten the whole Social Security ordeal and the imputed interest income mess. Oh well, I'll be fine after I take a couple of more laxatives.

To Give Feedback on the Course Itself

Once students were comfortable writing in their journals or e-mailing regularly, we both asked for entries that focused on what was happening in the class. Both of us appreciated students' candor when they had a private place to record their reactions to how the class was conducted. Journals provided us with windows on students' understanding, thinking, and satisfaction with the class. For example, a follow-up e-mail by Jane let Jerry know that his project explanation had been successful for her:

> I enjoyed your dog story today! How many times have I had a project in a class and I just keep dancing around it because it seems so huge and overwhelming? I think that is really a great allegory. It seems to be true of most projects in life, that we have a hard time seeing the trees for the forest. I very much ap-

preciate for that reason, that you are walking us through our projects a "piece of cookie" at a time. It saves on the feeling of being overwhelmed, and helps us to understand it at the same time.

Final Comments on Using Journals in Accounting Courses

As students become comfortable communicating with an instructor, typical barriers seem to disappear. We found formerly intimidating authority roles and formal scheduling are decreased because communication through journals can be ongoing and less constraining. If an instructor is a good responder, answering electronic or traditionally written journal messages in a timely and professionally personal fashion, then students often respond by increased writing and communicating.

After students received our responses (immediate from Jerry via a return e-mail) to their entries, the assignment increased in its meaningfulness. In Alan's class the day journals were returned, students read the responses with great enthusiasm. Alan noticed that his responses seemed to encourage more writing almost to the point where students wanted to write to see what his response would be. In a final entry Abby commented again how beneficial journals were for her:

> I really did enjoy writing in a journal this semester, especially in accounting. I thought that it was beneficial in many ways. First, I felt that if I had a problem or was confused on a concept, that I could express my feelings about it and not feel so dumb. Also, I have always felt that it is beneficial to write down ideas because then, you have the ability to see your ideas in front of your face. Once you write down something, read it and then reread it, I feel that it helps you understand it better. Also, I enjoyed the option that you weren't strict as to what topics we had to write about, nor that you corrected our grammar.

In Jerry's class students responded similarly about the benefits of the electronic journals, especially because they not only used them to write out their thinking and their questions, but also because Jerry responded promptly and kept the dialogue going. As Brad noted in one of his last e-mails of the term, "I am appreciative for the way you take time out to talk with students away from class. I realize you have a busy schedule, but you always make time for our questions. I am starting to look for career opportunities here on the Web, lots to learn." Jerry was right—the e-mail dialogue had increased his students' electronic proficiency, and from that relatively simple platform, students went on to use the technology in more varied forms. Thus, after our experience with journals the first time even though responding could become time-consuming, we will continue to use dialogue journal writing in some form with future accounting classes.

Works Cited

May, C. A. 1989. *Effective Writing: A Handbook for Accountants,* 2nd ed. Englewood Cliffs, NJ: Prentice-Hall.

Staton, J. 1987. "The Power of Responding in Dialogue Journals." In *The Journal Book,* ed. Toby Fulwiler, 47–63. Portsmouth, NH: Boynton/Cook Publishers.

Appendix A

ACCT 350 Intermediate Accounting I

Journal Assignment

Purpose of a Journal   Writing involves expressing one's thoughts in words, which in turn involves formulating and clarifying those thoughts. In this sense, writing is thinking. A journal, then, is a place to practice thinking.

Format Convention   Journal may be any of the following:

loose-leaf notebook

spiral or bound notebook

steno pad

Journal may be in pen, pencil, or word processed on one side of a page. Leave enough room on left margin (about 2 inches) for teacher responses.

Style of Writing   NO emphasis is placed on grammar, punctuation, and spelling.

Content   Teacher-selected—students write on same topic or list of topics provided.

Student selected—unfocused, whatever comes to mind.

Student selected—focused, topic in relation to the course content:

- one thing you learned from today's class,
- the main point of a lecture,
- one or more questions you still have about the topic discussed,
- a discovery you made as a result of the class reading,

Audience   Self + teacher + classmates (maybe)

Length of Entries   In time, ten to fifteen minutes max.

Frequency of Entries   Minimum of twice a week.

Time for Writing   In class and out of class.

Due Dates   Every other Thursday or Monday?

Sept 12	Sept 15
Sept 26	Sept 29
Oct 10	Oct 13
Oct 24	Oct 27
Nov 7	Nov 10
Nov 21	Nov 24
Dec 5	Dec 8

Responses from Teacher   As a real reader, not judgmental.

Appendix B

ACCT 467

Accounting Information Systems

Electronic Journal Assignment

Students are required to submit a weekly e-mail message to the instructor as a way of meeting the following objectives:

- Responding to material you are reading and experiencing in the course.
- Addressing issues of concern or interest to the student related to the course. The instructor will respond to all student concerns and issues relevant to the course curriculum.
- Communicating recommendations and suggestions to the instructor about the course. Students have a responsibility to make suggestions that improve the overall quality and experience of the course for future students.
- Improving written communication and developing an appreciation for communicating via e-mail.
- Developing your ability to generate ideas and recommendations.

Students who do not currently have an e-mail address will have one established in the computer lab. Students are required to submit a minimum of one electronic e-mail message per week. Makeup e-mail communications for weeks missed will not count. For purposes of grading this assignment, the week will commence on Friday 12:01 A.M. to Thursday 12:00 P.M. The electronic journal counts as 10% of the course grade.

11

Confronting Issues
Criminal Justice Students and Journal Writing

Michelle E. Heward, J.D., and Gary Dohrer, Ph.D.

I disagree with the book and I guess with the Supreme Court when they say that school children have little need for protection under the eighth amendment. I think they need that protection as much if not more than any adult. They are stating the openness of public schools and saying that a child could leave anytime he/she wanted to. This is simply not true. There are closed campuses and very often are instances where a student is placed alone with a teacher.

from a student journal

Can journal writing enhance the learning experience of Criminal Justice students? After a couple of years of teaching, Michelle found herself wanting to challenge her students more, make them more active in their learning experience, and better prepare them for work in the Criminal Justice field to challenge the institutions and the experts as the student above did. She met with Gary, the Director of the Writing-Across-the-Curriculum Program, who suggested using more focused writing, including journal writing in the classroom. Michelle approached the idea of using journals in her classes with some trepidation:

> Skeptical does not describe the feeling I had when I started looking at writing. Doesn't writing mean that all 150 plus students will be pouring in reams of paper? How can you critically review all of them? I was not prepared nor equipped to handle this type of increase in my teaching load. Isn't this some-

thing that the English department should do anyway? Isn't there a class some-where that manufactures good writers?

Despite her misgivings, Michelle did incorporate journal writing into an intro-ductory Criminal Justice class. This chapter discusses how she and Gary did it and what they learned.

Issues: Goals and Stumbling Blocks

Is writing important for all Criminal Justice students? Many of our students go on for advanced degrees in criminal justice, public administration, law, or re-lated fields. The benefits of good writing skills for those students are obvious. By far the majority of our students, however, become law enforcement officers, corrections officers, and criminologists. Do they need the same kind of writing experiences?

While we considered our students' needs, a seasoned police officer guest lectured in Michelle's introductory Criminal Law class. He asked the students to name the most valuable tool of an officer. Students guessed his gun, radio, training, handcuffs, and so forth. To everyone's surprise, he held up his pen. "Un-less I can write and express myself well, I will never be an effective officer." This guest's comments reinforced what Michelle knew as a former prosecutor: Officers must articulate themselves clearly in a report, or risk their credibility on the witness stand. Consider a police officer who fails to include in his report a piece of evidence that later becomes critical. Particularly in this "post-Furman" era, an officer's inaccurate or incomplete report leaves him open to the argu-ment that he later fabricated evidence.

Similarly, a corrections officer must persuade a judge or parole board that a recommended sentence is appropriate based upon the documentation she has compiled. Finally, a crime scene investigator or criminologist who gathers or analyzes evidence must accurately and systematically record her actions, test-ing procedures and findings.

When Michelle read written work from students, she became keenly aware of their writing weaknesses. Gary knew that often the initial impetus for faculty adopting journal strategies is to improve the writing of their students. However, Michelle was somewhat unusual in that she already used some writing in her classes and understood that students benefit from writing. She knew that writ-ing helps students clarify, understand, and learn the material better. Her moti-vation, then, was a bit different:

> I want to generate critical and individual thinking. I want to challenge my stu-dents to develop and express their own opinions, not adopt my views. I want them to read a case or an article, critically review the logic and reasoning, and draw their own conclusions. I want them to question and be creative in prob-lem solving.

So, two foci emerged. First, she wanted writing to enhance her students' learning experiences and second, she wanted to encourage good writing skills.

We began our move toward incorporating journals by examining the syllabus for Michelle's Criminal Law class. Immediately we noticed how generic it was. She required students to attend court and write about their experience. She also had students write their goals and expectations the first day of the course.

We discussed course objectives to see where journals could support them. We were confident we could design a series of directed journal writings to enrich class discussions and in turn the students' learning. The second concern, of teaching competent writers, presented another problem, although not an unusual one. Looking at Michelle's schedule of topics, we were both convinced that it was pretty crowded. Adding to the list of goals would compound an already existing time problem. She realized that some writing assignments were valuable for students processing course issues, but she was also painfully aware of the time she spent evaluating these exercises and was hesitant to add more writing exercises to her load. At that point, we began to investigate the functions a journal could play in improving writing, helping students confront course issues, while maintaining or reducing her paper load. What would these outside activities look like? How much time was Michelle willing or able to invest in setting up and processing these activities? How would they fit with the rest of the class material? The goal was not to add to the students' or Michelle's work, but to complement and supplement work they were already doing.

We carefully reviewed writing activities Michelle was already using, objectives of each, and how these objectives fit the course. Not wanting to lose the effectiveness of the projects she was already using, we looked for efficient ways to process them and ways to help students form writing habits they would see as a natural part of learning and practicing Criminal Justice.

Adding a Journal Assignment

We view a journal as a collection of students' writing, both directed and undirected. Write-to-learn activities allow students to explore and understand their own thinking about concepts from class, while directed writing experiences ask students to step outside their own thoughts, personalize and focus on issues they find compelling. Placing these together in the journal allows students to view their own reactions, interests, and questions side by side with the writings they collect. It also helps them review and revise their own thinking on class materials and concepts. Students can discover the growth and changes in their own ideas and judgments over the course of the term. As Megan wrote, "I found it [the journal] to be a great tool in helping me to organize the information gathered during this class. I found myself going the 'extra mile' in my reading and note taking, in order to come up with journal entries. This has translated into better test scores and a lot more retention on my part."

The concept of making writing a focus of Michelle's class was an exciting prospect. She required students to keep a three-ring binder with dividers as a journal so assignments could be easily pulled out, assessed, and returned. Some assignments would be handed in as the class progressed and then returned to students. Others could simply accumulate, to be reviewed along with the entire journal. Michelle also used a size limit of one-inch binders so she could carry several. Requiring typed or word processed assignments also cut down immensely on the time required for review.

Addition Equals Revision to the Syllabus

Michelle's syllabus changed dramatically to clarify her expectations. Although changes continue to be made, the following is the latest revised edition.

SYLLABUS

CRIMINAL LAW—CJ133
DR. MICHELLE E. HEWARD
COURSE DESCRIPTION

Surveys the American criminal justice system. Elements of crime, defenses, historical foundations, limits, purposes, and functions of the criminal justice system.

TEXT Criminal Law Principles and Cases Thomas J. Gardner
We will cover approximately one chapter per week and students should read ahead so they will be prepared to discuss the material covered in class.

ATTENDANCE
Attendance and class participation are important to the class. Attendance, or the lack thereof, will be a factor in determining your final grade. I am required to report absences of athletes, veterans, scholarship recipients, etc.

GRADING
Exams: There will be two exams, each of about equal weight. They will comprise approximately 80% of your grade.
Writing requirement: A journal is required for this course and will comprise approximately 20% of your grade. You will need a three-ring binder so that assignments can be easily removed and reinserted. I will periodically ask for particular assignments and on other occasions for your entire journal. The sections of the journal should be clearly divided with partitions as follows:

a. Court assignment. You are required to attend approximately two hours of a criminal court proceeding. After you attend court you will write two to three pages indicating 1) the type of matters that you saw in court (you do not need to include the defendant's names); 2) in detail the principles and vocabulary you learned in class that were used in court, and 3) most importantly, your personal thoughts about your court experience. How did the court handle the cases that came before it? Indicate things that surprised you, things that you agreed or disagreed with, and whether the experience was what you expected prior to taking this class.

b. Newspaper articles. Once a week, starting with the second week, you will find a newspaper article in a national or local paper of general circulation that deals with criminal law. Write a paragraph about the article, briefly explaining what it is about, what principles or terminology we have discussed in class that you saw in the article, any inconsistencies you saw in the article, and questions or comments it may have raised for you.

c. Reading/Discussion Questions: You will use the journal to record at least three questions or comments from the reading and class discussions on at least a weekly basis. These entries should be dated and will be used along with the newspaper articles for classroom discussion. You are encouraged to use this section of the journal to express questions you encounter about criminal law and to seek out the answers, or make comments about the material that will help you understand the material in a more meaningful way.

d. Lectures. Periodically throughout the course we will have outside speakers. You are required to make a journal entry prior to the speaker's attendance that sets forth at least three questions that you would like explored or discussed. This should help you focus and should encourage participation in the subject matter presented. After the speaker attends class, you will write your impressions on at least three topics covered by the speaker. This is *not* to be a recitation of what the speaker said, but your thoughts about the subject matter presented, whether you agreed or disagreed, or what you found interesting and why.

e. Miscellaneous. You should keep a section of your journal for miscellaneous items that may be assigned during the course of the class.

Remember, each journal entry must be clearly labeled to indicate the date and the name of the assignment. You may turn your assignments in for up to one week from the date it was due and receive late credit. No assignments will be received thereafter. All assignments must be typed except for the question/comment entries.

Directed Journal Activities

Michelle used the following assignments as directed journal writings for her Criminal Law class. Students were also encouraged to write about their own concerns, observations, questions, and hot points in their journals.

The Class Expectations Worksheet

One of Michelle's beginning assignments is her "Class Expectations Work-sheet," which asks the following questions:

Name:

Telephone number:

E-mail address:

Class standing (circle): Freshman   Sophomore   Junior   Senior   Grad

Major field of study:

Why are you taking this class?

What areas of criminal law would you like to cover in this class if we can work it in?

Are you currently employed, or have you been employed, in an area related to the law? If so, please explain.

Are there any special needs that you may have that I should be aware of as your instructor?

This worksheet saves class time, and Michelle receives candid answers from students. In one instance she became aware of a student requiring special accommodations as a result of a disability. The worksheet also helps her deter-mine the classes' experience with the subject matter and their expectations for the class. Students benefited from thinking about what they wanted to learn from the class as well. It took less than a minute for Michelle to review each paper, and the exercise seems to start the class on a positive note since students realize she takes a genuine interest in them.

Michelle was also able to learn about the class composition from this first writing. She has a lot of law enforcement and correctional officers in her classes. Many of them have vast experience in the practical aspects of criminal law. Knowing students' backgrounds helps her meet their differing educational needs effectively and use their talents in class. Since the course curriculum al-lows her some flexibility to cover different aspects of criminal law, this exercise helps her accommodate students' particular interests. This introductory journal activity provides important information without taking valuable class time.

Visiting and Analyzing Criminal Court

Another successful directed journal assignment involves students attending a criminal court and writing their findings. The goal of this assignment is to give students practical experience seeing the criminal justice system in action and, thus, reinforce class material. More importantly, the writing helps students analyze their personal thoughts about the system, how it works, and how it could be improved. Marty, an articulate journal-writing student, described his reaction to the court visit as follows:

> Aside from the physical part of the courtroom, things seemed to move along fairly efficiently. In two hours they disposed of almost twenty cases. I guess the one impression I got was that things were a lot more informal than I had envisioned. There were a lot of lawyers that were coming and going and things got fairly disorganized, again, not how it was depicted on Night Court.
>
> Overall, I found my first day in court to be very enlightening. I think everyone should have to spend some time in a courtroom in order to gain an understanding of our legal system . . . I found it to be a great way to top off this class as well as reinforce the new information gained in it.

Although students "book learn" the system, no substitute exists that can duplicate practical experience like this. Many students indicated surprise at seeing so much happening in court, expecting a more serene, churchlike atmosphere. Others expressed discomfort seeing someone shackled or incarcerated for a violent felony. For most, this visit was the first time they had been in court, thus opening their eyes to an important part of government. Many said they wanted to go back again on their own time. In her course evaluation, Kimberly commented, "My favorite writing assignment was the court assignment. It did spark interest." Luann, a student who works as an officer in the justice system said, ". . . the court assignment helped me the most." Lisa stated, "I enjoyed this assignment tremendously, to the point I have once again evaluated my career choices and believe that I would enjoy playing a role in the criminal court system."

Michelle used the student observations and conclusions to lead a good class discussion and to clarify material previously covered in class. In addition, since students asked questions in their journal entries, much dialogue occurred with Michelle—outside class. One thing Michelle learned from assigning the court visit was to clearly explain her expectations for the journal. Students reciting what they saw in court is not educational for them, nor is it beneficial for the instructor. What Michelle reemphasized is the importance of the analysis of their experience.

Michelle encourages students to turn the assignment in as soon as they go to court so papers do not all come in to her at once, and when she returns them, students can put them back in their journals. With a two-page limit, these entries take less than a couple of minutes per paper to review. She responds most often by posing questions or expressing interest in what they saw.

Newspaper Coverage of a Criminal Case

Another specific entry Michelle asks students to write during the term is the newspaper assignment. This assignment initially requires students to read a newspaper for one week and pull out three articles discussing a criminal case they find interesting, confusing, or compelling. They then write a paragraph, detailing reasons they picked the article, questions it raised, terminology from class they noted in the article, or other points of interest. As a result of student feedback, Michelle is now requiring this assignment once a week.

The goal of this assignment is to help students become good media consumers. There is an overabundance of criminal law-related articles in any newspaper. Every student in this class should be able to not only understand but be critical of news reports regarding the criminal justice system.

In evaluations students indicated the assignment was helpful. Brian commented, "The newspaper writing requirements . . . gave me the opportunity to learn about real stuff." Unfortunately many students do not read the newspaper on a regular basis, and this assignment helped to pique their interest. Brandon added, "I feel the newspaper assignment helped me the most. I actually got more involved with what was going on in the community." Michelle did not comment much on these directed journal assignments, and, thus, it did not take long to review each entry. Often, however, students asked questions arising from the newspaper articles, many of which she could address in class discussion. For example, after reading an article on a liability case involving an animal attack, Kaycee wrote, "As I was doing the newspaper assignment, I had some questions. How does someone become a judge? Can an animal owner be responsible for the animal's actions? To what degree?" Again, for this assignment to be worthwhile, students must clearly understand they need to analyze their thoughts about the article and not simply paraphrase it.

Reflecting on Issues Presented by Guest Speakers

Guest lectures provide another directed journal assignment. Prior to guest lectures, students make a journal entry with three questions for the speaker. After the lecture, in one to two pages, students describe their personal opinions on three issues the speaker presented.

Because this introductory class surveys various areas of the criminal justice system, Michelle dedicates approximately four class periods to guest lectures chosen according to class interests. Before she initiated some writing prior to guests coming in, lectures sometimes became a time for students to passively sit back and listen. Writing out questions prepared students for the lectures and often helped lecturers understand students' interests.

For example, while preparing for a guest attorney, Kaycee wrote the following question: "As a defense attorney, how do you feel justice is served when a defendant confesses crimes to you? Then you in turn, knowing they are guilty, try to get a not-guilty verdict?" The lecturer was able to direct his remarks to this particular concern, and Kaycee actively listened for the answer to her question.

Michelle has found this particular journal assignment has been beneficial in assessing which lectures the students enjoyed and which should not be repeated. Most importantly, writing this journal entry requires students to take part in the lecture, thinking about the topic ahead of time and afterwards. Students have to analyze their own thoughts and form their own opinions. Sean, a family counseling major, said, "I enjoyed writing on the different speakers because it made me think. I put more thought into what they had said."

After a lecture by a prosecutor, students expressed how much they learned from him that they had never even considered before. Anne commented, "reports on speakers . . . made you pay attention and participate" Lonnie reinforced this idea, "Knowing I had to write about the topic made me more attentive. Liked how you told us to write about our own thoughts, not just what the speaker stated." Students clearly enjoyed the challenge of exploring their own opinions. The students could later review both their questions and reactions reinforcing those concepts learned during the lecture. To Michelle's delight, she has had several students express themselves in unique ways. Klint, for example, used a poem, "Invictus" by William Henley, to reflect his thoughts about a police officer who spoke to the class about a fatal shooting he was involved in.

Writing to Learn Journal Assignments

Michelle incorporates a number of other writing assignments into the journal. One she uses periodically to assess students' understanding after a difficult lecture. She ends the class about five minutes early and asks them to write any points from the lecture that were unclear. The response is extremely helpful, and she is able to prepare the next lecture by going over the unclear points and building upon those points students understand. This assessment helps her avoid covering material unnecessarily a second time, assuming students did not understand it, and allows her to focus her efforts on unclear concepts. Melinda, a criminal justice major, wrote, "It [the journal entry] is helpful. We really had to think about what we were learning. It was especially beneficial if we weren't understanding a concept." Michelle assures students they do not have to come up with an unclear point if they actually understand the material.

She has also used journal assignments to urge students to form opinions about a particular subject prior to talking about it in class. One assignment focused students by having them set up their own criminal justice system. She has found that class participation is greater and better informed when students have done these assignments. When the class discusses this material, the students are prepared and have formed opinions. In these journal writes Michelle has noticed students coming to a conclusion about a concept. For example, after writing up her own criminal justice system, Kaycee commented, "I guess I've always taken for granted that we have a good system in the U.S. It's easy to criticize our system or any other system when I am not the one to reform or find solutions to the problems."

In one class a student said that he would make sentences uniform for everyone; everyone who committed a particular act would receive the same punishment. This comment led to an important class discussion on individualized punishment, and through their writing students were prepared enough so that discussion was carried by the class with little involvement from Michelle. On another occasion a student said that she would not incarcerate anyone unless he or she had committed a violent crime against a person—again, leading to a thought-provoking discussion on alternative sentencing options.

Michelle has students make three journal entries per week regarding questions or comments they have either from class material and the text, or from some other source, regarding criminal law. This activity evoked the following comment from Robin, "The questions helped because they made me think." Brian agreed, "[They] helped me remember what we had learned in class." Finally, Jenny added, "Journal writing was good for me because I had all of these things going on in my head regarding the laws and crime and how I and my family fit in; writing it down helps me to reflect later."

What Happened When We Used
These Assignments

The advantages of Michelle's foray into using journals have been many. The level of interaction with her students, which has increased, is both personally fulfilling and intellectually stimulating. Students have responded with doubts about whether they could handle a particular job, or excitement about discovering an interest.

Students' journals allowed Michelle to better understand students and their needs. She had a particular student who had been the victim of a violent sexual assault. Being aware of this helped Michelle understand the student's feelings regarding the way the justice system treats victims. When students think things out and draw their own conclusions, their learning is enhanced.

Through their journals, students were able to see writing as a tool for their own learning. At the end of the term they have the journal to review material and discover how much writing they have done—an accomplishment for many of them who are not used to writing. They can measure their learning by seeing their contrasting views expressed over the course of the term.

By writing, students are forced to carefully review their own opinions. If the opinions are only in their heads, they are more easily changed. If students write down their opinions, they have to make the opinions their own. Students also have an opportunity to review their ideas and their analysis and see if they make sense or if they change. Ideas recorded in journals are more accessible and salient than mental concepts. Val expressed the following, "They [writing assignments] helped me to rethink my first opinions I wrote. When you read what you think, you can see if it's logical or silly. I think it does stimulate thought processes, and brings up new ideas, and questions."

Assessing What We Have Learned

Journal writing in a Criminal Justice course enriches the learning experience for both students and instructor. We have, however, four observations and cautions:

1. Clearly set forth expectations.
2. Frequently encourage and remind students about their journal entries.
3. Help students connect their journal writing with learning and the processing of class concepts so their responses become an integral part of the class.
4. Do not bite off more than can be effectively and efficiently handled.

Clear Expectations Equal Less Frustration

Simply and clearly setting forth expectations avoids frustration and disappointment. Journal writing requires introspection and personal expression; students may be reluctant to express their personal thoughts unless it is expected and connected to their learning. We suggest not only clearly articulating expectations in writing but also the goals of the journal writing, enabling students to envision what the instructor hopes to accomplish. At midterm, when Michelle first called for the journals, students were doing what they had been asked to do—they were making entries. Many entries showed little thought or personal expression. After an explanation of why she wanted the entries made and what her goals were, students began using the journals much more effectively.

Frequent Use of Journals Make Entries Important

Students must be reminded to make their journal entries and must see those journal entries used as part of the classroom discussion. Michelle became excited about journal writing, incorporating it into all of her classes. In one particular class, however, she simply put it in the syllabus, requiring the students to make at least three journal entries per week. She then made no further mention of the journal. Toward the end of the class, someone asked if she was going to call for the journals. To her surprise she found that about a third of the students had kept the journal without any encouragement, although that figure may be somewhat enhanced by students who were willing to make entries after the fact simply to get points for an assignment. Not surprisingly, the students did not have a positive experience with journal writing. When asked what they disliked about the class or what they would change, Kristine, a senior student, commented, "[The journal writing was] not helpful, I just did it to get the grade. . . . Writing out questions every week was sometimes tedious."

The journal-writing assignment was less successful because expectations were not clearly set forth, students were not reminded about their entries, nor were journals used in class. Not surprisingly, students saw journal writing as busy work, the very thing Michelle wanted to avoid. Sara suggested, "One question at the end of each brief would encourage students to critically examine the issues more." Michelle has now incorporated journal writing as part of the brief-writing assignment, asking students to personalize their brief and think about the decision in terms of their own sense of justice. This assignment will prepare students for classroom discussions and require personal introspection.

Connecting Journal Writing to Course Learning Pays Off

The class described above is in stark contrast to her Criminal Law class where she made a conscientious effort to use student journal entries in the class. The evaluations from the students were markedly different. Andy indicated, "It [journal writing] gets you thinking, not just reading the chapter." Stephanie, a young energetic student noted, "I found journal writing very helpful. I noticed that when I wrote down things I remembered them a lot better; knowing I had to write three questions made me think about questions where before, I wouldn't bother questioning even if I didn't understand the material." Marty summarized his journal-writing experience,

> I found it to be a great tool in helping me to organize the information gathered during the class. I found myself going the 'extra mile' in my reading and note taking, in order to come up with journal entries. This translated into better test scores and a lot more retention on my part.

Even when Michelle made a conscientious effort to encourage the journal writing, she found she was not using it in the classroom enough. Although most students enjoyed the journal-writing process, there were still some who resisted. Again, it appears that some students needed to see more connection with class material while others used the journal writing as a self-motivating tool. Michelle is considering two changes to her syllabus. First, students will write about a current news event involving criminal law once a week instead of once during the term. Second, she will devote a portion of the class each week to answering questions students have raised about material she is covering as well as those surfacing from their journal entries. Hopefully these uses will further diminish the small minority of students who did not connect with this assignment.

Moderation Is Key to Journal Assignments

Finally, the last caution is not to bite off more than can be effectively and efficiently handled. Using journals can be demanding. Organization and preparation are necessary to keep papers in order. Michelle notes, "As an attorney I never pushed as much paper as I do as a professor." Having students keep a journal has cut down Michelle's paper load, although it is still a significant time commitment. Because journal writing is such a wonderful tool, she finds herself engrossed in what the students are finding helpful and interesting. We suggest to teachers wanting to include journals in their classes to choose one class at a time initially. Experience with integrating journals in one class allows teachers to get a feel for the time commitment involved.

Final Thoughts

In working together and reviewing student evaluations of the journal component, we believe that Michelle reached her goal in showing students that writing can be effectively used as a communication and thinking tool. In addition, she has convinced herself that writing is a highly effective learning tool for many students in her Criminal Justice courses. Whether students were asked to write about their visit to a criminal court, analyze the treatment of a criminal case in the news media, prepare and then react to a guest lecturer, or make some other type of journal entry, each time they wrote they had to think about and confront the issues being raised in the course. Another plus for journal writing is simply the practice with writing this assignment provides. As students become more used to writing, Michelle has noticed many have become more proficient writers. This journal-writing experience, she hopes, will help prepare them for the kind of writing they will encounter as Criminal Justice professionals.

12

Distinguishing Between Fact and Opinion
Journals in a Legal Assistant Program

Kelly De Hill, J.D.

I sat down and read my journal this morning and it has been a very good exposé of my experiences this semester. I am amazed how much I have learned and especially observed that has been of value this quarter simply because I have had to write it down to complete the journal entry requirement. The way my mind works sometimes surprises me immensely.

Helena

Perhaps you have heard of legal assistants or perhaps you know the profession by the name *paralegal*. I first saw the term several years ago in an advertisement in the back of a women's magazine; it read "Be a paralegal! Get your certificate by mail!" The ad gave me the idea the profession was one performed with ease and was somehow suspect. I now know differently.

Beginnings of the Paralegal Profession

Because the paralegal profession evolved from the legal secretary profession, lawyers viewed it as an amplified secretarial position—a secretary with more responsibility and more client contact perhaps, but a secretary nonetheless. As the profession grew, paralegals began performing more specialized tasks. They assisted lawyers in preparing for trial by summarizing depositions, preparing trial notebooks, gathering and organizing information acquired in discovery, preparing discovery requests, responding to discovery requests, and attending trials and hearings. Legal assistants became more involved with clients, often conducting intake interviews or writing informational letters. They began to interview witnesses and conduct investigations. Lawyers realized that unlike secretaries, who are considered part of overhead costs, well-trained paralegals could actually create profit for the firm.

The early '80s seemed to be a time of unending and expanding litigation, and the paralegal profession exploded as lawyers recognized the need for trained assistants. Few paralegals, however, performed many writing tasks in their workplace. Attorneys and law clerks did most of the research and nearly all the writing; secretaries did the typing.

Then the personal computer arrived. Legal assistants who had avoided typing because they were trying to be seen as different from the secretarial support in the firms now needed to be computer literate. Personal computers would eventually sit on everyone's desk, senior partners as well associate attorneys, and everyone engaged in "typing."

In addition to the personal computer, the late '80s and the early '90s witnessed an insistent demand for less expensive ways to access the justice system. Corporations brought their litigation in-house and hired attorneys as employees to avoid paying outrageous hourly fees. Insurance companies and businesses insisted that law firms use legal assistants more extensively. Clients refused to pay for billable hours that were charged at the attorney rate when a legal assistant could have accomplished the task at a lower rate.

Law firms became interested in devising ways to save their clients money. One strategy was to assign paralegals more of the tasks traditionally reserved for lawyers. Instead of simply typing or filing documents, paralegals began to write complaints, answer discovery questions, research questions of law, draw up contracts, compose legal briefs to the court, and write letters—all at a lower fee.

The combination of these factors—personal computers, expanded use of legal assistants, and demand for quality work at lower rates—resulted in a need for legal assistants who were able to do more than fill out forms and checklists. Law firms and corporate legal departments needed paralegals who could research, analyze, summarize, and organize information, concepts, facts, and theories—in short, perform the tasks associated with and required for good writing.

Writing in the Legal Assistant Program

The legal assistant program at Westminster College is an intensive and intellectually demanding eleven-month program. The program has a strong emphasis on writing and research—two areas of law that used to belong exclusively to law clerks or attorneys. Writing and research makes our program unique from other training programs and I believe, as the director, gives Westminster graduates a professional edge. Our program is approved by the American Bar Association and the employment placement rate is above 90 percent. Graduates of our program work in insurance companies, hospitals, corporate legal departments, government agencies, and human resource departments. Some of them have bachelor's degrees, some have master's degrees, and some have no college training at all when they arrive in our program. With few exceptions, when they graduate, they can write well, analyze carefully, and solve problems thoughtfully.

Good legal writing requires that the writer have a very clear understanding of the differences between questions of law, questions of fact, legal argument, and personal opinion. Getting students to understand these concepts and the place of each in legal writing is the real battle. As Hollis Hurd states in *Writing for Lawyers* (1982),

> Lawyers think differently from normal people. The key to writing for lawyers is to give them what their specialized mode of thought needs. This is a special skill which every paralegal, law student and young lawyer needs to learn, because writing which is good—or even superb—in other contexts such as literary or commercial will often be bad legal writing.

Because the students in the legal assistant program undergo a rather stringent admissions process, all of them can put together a grammatically correct sentence and a reasonable paragraph. Most understand the concept of a beginning, a middle, and an end. Although they struggle, as many adult writers do, with issues of organization, most of our legal assistant students enjoy writing and consider themselves fairly good, if not excellent, writers. However, their idea of a legal argument is, often, in summary, "because I think so." I needed a tool: a way that students could feel the difference between making an argument based on fact and the law and one based on personal opinion.

Using Informal Writing in a Paralegal Seminar

In 1993, I added a required journal-writing component in a class entitled Professional Practice and Ethics, a course that students take in the second semester of the program. Designed as a seminar, the course features a guest lecturer each week on topics that are essential to a successful career as a legal assistant. The fourteen-week course is divided into two sections. The first section focuses on the day-to-day aspects of being a paralegal such as office politics, tracking billable hours, interfacing with attorneys, and dealing with the ethical dilemmas that arise in law. The second section focuses on how to land a job. Students attend presentations on résumé writing and interviewing skills. They are videotaped doing a mock interview, and a panel of attorneys and current legal assistants reviews their résumés. The class requires students to delve into personal evaluation and to form opinions about matters for which there are no black-and-white, right-or-wrong resolutions. Requiring a journal for this class was a natural extension of the self-evaluation requirements already in place.

The purpose of the course, described in the syllabus, is as follows:

> As the legal assistant profession and the program at Westminster has grown and matured, it has become clear that our graduates, in order to be more marketable and more successful, require training in the professional and practical aspects of finding a job and succeeding in that job.
>
> In an increasingly difficult job market, professional training from an excellent program is not enough. Legal assistant candidates must learn how to showcase their unique abilities and to present themselves, in paper and in person, as knowledgeable professionals ready to take on challenging tasks.
>
> The purpose of this course is to provide students with the opportunity to explore ways and means of surviving with dignity and grace the ordeal of getting a job and keeping it.

I introduce the journal requirement on the first night of class and give the class the following handout:

RESPONSE JOURNAL

Procedure:

During the presentation, take notes, jot down questions, think about the material being presented. After the presentation, write your responses to what you just heard, observed, or read. Fill up a page or two. Think of this writing as informal and for discovery—no need to worry about form and style. You want to start ideas simmering in your head about the presentation. These responses will be particularly helpful as you prepare your cover letter, résumé, and final writing assignment.

Do not fall behind in your journal because it will become meaningless to you. It would be a good idea if you developed the habit of bringing your journal with you to class. Then, you will not forget it at those times when it is due to be handed in.

Purpose:

1. To help you respond actively to the information.
2. To help you remember and understand the information.
3. To give you a tool for self-evaluation.
4. To help you generate ideas on paper.
5. To improve your writing fluency.

Audience:

Primarily yourself. But I will be reviewing it.

Strategies for Writing Quality Responses:

1. Write personally. Be yourself. There will be "I" references in your responses. Be frank in your response.

2. Write fully. Say enough to take up and explore your reactions in some detail.

3. Become engaged. Move beyond summarizing the information. Write about how the information affected you and whether it will affect your behavior or thoughts in the future.

4. Ask questions. Propose a plan of action.

5. Make connections. What did the presentation or the information call to mind? Have you had experiences similar to that of the presenter?

6. Speculate. Consider alternative possibilities and interpretations.

Possible Response Topics:

The following list provides suggested topics if you need a starting point for your writing. They are only suggestions; you are not limited to using them. If you do refer to this list before writing your responses, please avoid using the same focus for each entry.

-   Tell how you feel about the presentation and the information presented.

-   Write about any difficulties or frustrations.

-   Write about something you do not understand.

-   Write about the way this presentation confirms or confronts your beliefs.

-   Write about something in the presentation that reminded you of someone you know or of something that has happened in your life.

-   Write about an idea expressed in class with which you agree or disagree.

-   Write about something new you learned.

-   Write about an experience you had after acting upon the information presented.

And finally . . .

Feel free to write about any of the classes in the program, what you are learning, how it is affecting you. You may also write about your life outside your legal studies, but do not feel compelled to do so. Who knows? You may come to enjoy journal writing so much that you begin keeping a personal journal just for you in addition to the response journal you are using for this class!

Rather than require an entry every day or so, I ask the students to hand in a total amount of entries, depending upon the grade they are seeking. I specifically state that I am not interested in lists or a rundown of everything that happens on a given day but want to read their thoughts and why they think the way they do. I explain that becoming a good writer requires practice and every opportunity for writing of any kind counts as practice.

Although many had kept a diary of some sort in the past and some had been required to write in a journal in high school, keeping a journal as part of a college class requirement was, for most of them, a new idea. They did not like the idea. Because the legal assistant program is a professional course, the students arrive focused on the practical. Many of them have been working in law offices, and they know the value of tasks that can count as billable hours. When I introduced the assignment, the students often felt that with all the homework and writing required by the other classes, taking valuable study time to "explore, discover, and so on" via a journal not graded for style, grammar, or content was a waste of time. In fact, many of the students were rather hostile.

As students voiced their objections, I realized they often view introspection as an impractical endeavor and that, in order for the journal assignment to be successful, students must understand the assignment in the context of the legal world. Before giving them the journal assignment, I tell them about my experience with an attorney who attempted to use his personal view of my client as a legal argument. The case involved the breakup of a long marriage that, by all accounts, had been happy for several years. The parties could not agree on the division of marital property or on a visitation schedule for their young children. A hearing was set before the Domestic Commissioner. At the hearing, the attorney for the husband argued that my client, the wife, was being unreasonable, unfair, and irrational because she was having emotional problems due to her grief and denial of the end of the marriage, and so the court should rule in favor of the husband. I objected on the grounds that opposing counsel's personal opinion of my client's state of mind was irrelevant and that he failed to present any factual basis for his proposal for property division and visitation. The Domestic Commissioner upheld my objection and, visibly annoyed with opposing counsel, instructed him to focus on the facts of the case and to keep his personal opinions about my client out of his presentation.

At the end of this story, I ask the class for their response. Many want to know if the husband's attorney was correct in his assumptions about my client. Most do not understand how and why the attorney's personal view had no bearing on the facts of the case. I am able to use this story as an example of a legal professional who, because of his inability to see the difference between his personal opinion and the facts, was unable to make an effective and persuasive argument for his client. The class and I discuss how our emotional perspective certainly influences and colors our views of the facts, but we need to be able to acknowledge when this occurs and to be careful that we do not mistake our personal viewpoint for an objective fact.

Building on this dicussion, I introduce the journal assignment as a means for them to begin to fine tune their ability to differentiate between opinions, emotions, and facts. Writing in a journal in the personal format complements their other writing courses where they must write primarily in the objective format. As a result, I tell them, they will become better writers overall.

Helping Students See the Legal Power of Journals

Although I hope that, as the students write in their journals, they will see, understand, and treasure the intrinsic value of journal keeping, I do not underestimate their love of things legal. And so, in an effort to combat the students' sense that this informal, unstructured writing is not important, I cite several examples of the use and power of journals as evidence.

A Journal as Evidence in a Divorce Case

For my first example I describe a case where I represented a man whose wife, a teacher at the state prison, wanted a divorce because she was having a secret affair with an inmate who was her student. It was a relatively simple divorce because she wanted my client to have physical custody of the children, she did not want the house, and he was willing to be generous in the division of the marriage's financial assets. A few weeks after the divorce was final, my client called to give me his ex-wife's and her inmate lover's journals. Many inmates kept journals as a writing tool in classes and as part of their therapy in learning to manage their feelings effectively. They would write and the teachers would respond. The teacher/ex-wife, however, had abused the journal assignment by using it to carry on her romance with her student.

Her employer had learned of allegations of the affair, which was against both school and prison policies, and had removed her from the classroom pending the outcome of an investigation. The ex-wife had threatened to kill her supervisor, left the prison, driven to the home of my client, and tried to take the children away with her. My client convinced her to allow him to take her to a hospital instead. On the way, she confessed to him that she had taken the journals from the prison, and she turned them over to him "for protection." Once he had them, the sheriff's office, the county attorney's office, the school district, and prison officials were all calling him to turn over the journals to them because they were "evidence." The journals could be used to support terminating the ex-wife, extending the prison term of the inmate, or even eliminating the prison education program.

A Journal as Evidence to Help Establish Paternity

As a second example, I use a case where the state was trying to establish the paternity of a child and get an order for child support from the alleged father. The alleged father and the mother stated different time periods for their relationship.

He argued that, based upon the birthday of the child, the child could not be his because he was involved with the mother in the winter. The mother testified that their relationship occured in the spring, and she had written in her journal about their relationship. The judge allowed the journal entries to be considered as evidence because the entries were written at the time of the alleged events and added credibility to the mother's version of the facts.

A Journal as Damaging Evidence

My third example is the scandal that erupted when Senator Bob Packwood was accused of sexual harassment and eventually forced out of the U.S. Senate. According to various news reports, the complainant had charged that she was not the only woman harassed by him. She claimed Senator Packwood had a long history and pattern of sexually harassing the women in his office. Packwood tried to defend himself by submitting journal entries that he claimed showed that he was not harassing any of the women named. However, he refused to give the Senate Committee the entire journal. It was later discovered that Packwood had altered the entries he submitted.

While these stories impress the students with the potential power of journals, their first few entries show some remained unconvinced that journal writing would have any value for them. For example, Kasey wrote:

> When I first heard that we had to write this journal, I thought what a waste of precious time. I still haven't made up my mind about this, but I still am not for this idea. I know that it doesn't take all that much time to write an entry, but with all the commitments that I have, anything that impedes on the scarce free time I have is an inconvenience . . . We'll see how it goes.

A few students, as shown in Taylor's entry, grasped the concept from the beginning and welcomed the opportunity to write without editing:

> Ok. Here goes. I have never kept a journal. When I was young I loved the idea of keeping a diary. The only problem was I didn't want to do the writing. I wanted to open the diary or journal and have all these exciting entries just jump out at me. What an exciting life I lead, look at all the interesting things I've accomplished. Unfortunately, since I would be the one doing the writing and I wasn't very good at writing interesting or exciting things, nor would I readily write down my thoughts or ideas, it was a silly concept that obviously didn't work out. So here I am as an adult with journal entries to write for school. Everyone moaned and groaned about keeping the journal. But I do see the point. The only way to be a confident, fluid writer is to write. And all forms of writing will just increase our writing confidence and skill, both for the job market and possibly to make us into private journal keepers, ha!

What I Hoped Journal Writing Would Accomplish

In deciding to introduce journal keeping into the program, I had three primary goals for the assignment. First, I wanted to help the students develop a sense of the personal so that they could *feel* when they were lapsing into the personal when, in fact, a writing assignment required objectivity and arguments unrelated to their own emotions or ideas. Second, journals would give students the opportunity to analyze their learning experience, including the teachers and the curriculum in a safe forum. Using informal writing about their learning, I hoped, would polish their analytical skills and improve the quality of their structured legal writing assignments. Finally, I knew that by being forced to just write, without worrying about grammar and spelling, their overall writing would improve.

In addition to overseeing the Professional Practice and Ethics course, I taught Legal Writing II in the same semester and had many of the same students. In Legal Writing II, the assignments are formal and, consequently, I don't assign a journal. The students write interoffice memoranda, case briefs, letters, and memoranda in support of various motions to the court for an audience of supervising attorneys, clients, or judges.

As I read the journals from the Professional Practice class, I found that some students used their journals to communicate with me about their writing assignments in Legal Writing II or to talk about their writing process. For instance, Suzette wrote, "Legal Writing II is a lot harder than the first writing class. I'm glad that you spent the time to review the differences between facts and opinions. That concept is hard to grasp. The assignment of a letter to a client is going to be hard for me."

In one of his entries, Scott described his writing process:

> I find that if I have the basics of any process I can get through the problem. If I try to skip some steps or try to start in the middle, I have nothing but trouble. I do this skipping of steps especially in writing and reading. I need to slow down and remind myself that you don't get extra points for being the first one done. What I have started to do is use IRAC more in my writing process. I also find that if I write while I'm reading, I remember more. I am having an interesting time working on the memorandum of law for Legal Writing II. I seem to be at the point with this writing where I know enough to be uncomfortable about not putting enough information in it. On the other hand, I don't know enough to know if any other issues need to be addressed. I would like this nice little concise box of directions which tells me what goes where. Unfortunately, writing doesn't work that way.

Lynda also used her journal to discuss her writing:

> We had our case briefs in *Gnerre* and *Mueller* returned to us in Legal Writing II. It's interesting to me that my writing wasn't as focused in *Gnerre,* which

was a much shorter, seemingly easier to understand case than *Mueller.* I had to read *Mueller* several times before I felt like I understood exactly what was going on. Apparently, the extra readings helped; my work was much better on that one. The case brief assignments are a good exercise in analyzing what you read. I have always been such a voracious reader that sometimes I read too quickly and don't really digest what is being taken in. It's good for me to step back and ask some questions of myself about what I'm reading. I really like this stuff!

Occasionally, Suzette would use some of her journal entries to pose grammar questions. "A question for you re: legal writing. Is it true that we can never use contractions, such as 'I'll,' 'I'm,' etc.? In Legal Writing I, we were not allowed to use them and I find myself slipping up, on occasion. I realize that it is proper not to use them when addressing the court, but how about an internal memo to your supervising attorney?"

Because I read their writing in both Legal Writing II and the Professional Practice/Ethics course, I was able to see firsthand that their writing did improve as they became more aware of their own writing. Taylor noted in her last entry:

This is my last entry. And yes, it's true; it has gotten easier for me to just sit down and write. I am not nearly as self-conscious about writing extemporaneously as I used to be. Unfortunately, as I re-read my journal entries, I am not entirely pleased with my writing style. Since I know that this is not a formal assignment I have a very casual approach and almost a cavalier use of language. I would like to be more colorful in the sense that I want someone to be able to read what I wrote and visualize a picture. I also think I need to work on connective language. I found myself starting and stopping with no transitions.

The act of writing in two very different contexts, often in the same night, I believe, assisted the students in seeing, feeling, and understanding the difference between informal and formal, personal and objective. Several of the students' journal entries reflected this newly discovered ability to step out of the emotional arena and deal with just the facts. Kathi wrote in her journal about how she was dealing better with an extended family member because she was learning to focus on the facts:

I think I did a much better job at hearing what Mary Evelyn was saying and what her concerns were. Mind you, I still think she's not taking responsibility for herself and her own actions, but that is beside the point. I think I needed to really hear and she needed to be heard. I think the methods used by attorneys which you have discussed are starting to make a difference in the way I deal with people. It makes it easier to get at the real issue, rather than losing sight of the real problem with emotionalism.

The Unexpected Outcomes of Journal Writing

While I believe that the journal assignment achieved my main goals, some outcomes I did not expect. Students reported higher satisfaction with the Professional Practice/Ethics course because the journal writing helped them to retain and internalize the information. As I counseled with individual students later regarding their job search, they seemed more focused and thoughtful. Several would openly refer to their journal, saying "as I wrote you in my journal" or "I discussed this in my journal last semester."

Another feature of the journal was the open communication beyond the assignment that occurred. Sometimes students would use their journals to "talk" to me as the director of the legal assistant program about a teacher or an assignment. I learned more about what or who was effective in the program from their journals than I would have ever gleaned from going over course evaluations. As a result of the comments written in their journals, I was able to make adjustments, counsel with teachers, and plan the future direction of the program more confidently.

The journal assignment also gave me the opportunity to individually respond to each student. Several stated they looked forward to my comments. They felt heard. I had not foreseen that the journal entries and my response would be a bonding mechanism. Because students knew I read their journals, they were often more comfortable about discussing difficult, but important, issues and matters of concern with me. I, in turn, was more patient and more helpful to them because of the opportunity to glimpse the world through their perspective.

The greatest unforeseen outcome was the assistance the journal gave the students in keeping their emotional balance. People who attend our program and want to be legal assistants love detail and crave organization. They are frequently intense, driven, competitive, and obsessive. They are intelligent and talented. They love studying and working with the law. But as they go through the program with like-minded souls, often while working full-time during the day and tending to family responsibilities in the evening, they can make themselves, their loved ones, their teachers, and each other crazy.

Although the students are grown-ups, they have a tendency to regress into typical student behavior as a result of finding themselves in a desk, having to raise their hands, and perform in a context over which they have no control. Full-time students in this program spend three evenings a week, in four- to five-hour blocks, with each other for forty-two continuous weeks. Then they spend time together outside of the classroom in the law library and working in study groups. Of course, they find themselves a bit irritable and short-tempered. I found myself counseling students, mediating conflicts, and trying to help them keep their perspective and their focus as they worked their way toward graduation. I discovered, however, the journal helped the students focus on their goals, remain motivated, and express their frustration in an effective and safe manner. As Kathi wrote:

> The people who fail, week after week, to provide any help to others and ask only for the answers (ask is not the right word at this point—it's demand or expect) are the ones who have my hair on end. I think this recital is another symptom of the "frantic finals phenomenon." We started griping and picking at each other in December, didn't we? We're doing it again, aren't we? Okay, if I recognize it, I can deal with it better. Good idea to write journals.

Kasey, who was skeptical about the journal assignment in the beginning, acknowledged its value:

> It's funny. I just looked back over some of my journal entries and I have really used this journal to get all of my anger out. I don't know if that was the purpose—but it did help me to vent. I have noticed, in the last few days, that I am relaxing quite a bit and things aren't so bad anymore. I think I came to terms with myself that I won't be considered a failure if I don't get straight A's and it's okay to do your best, but not to be insane about it.

Journal Writing—A Valuable Assignment in Paralegal Education

It is ironic that although students are, in the beginning, uncomfortable with the *introspection* piece of journal writing, as the assignment continues, reflection is the part they come to value the most. Entries like Corinne's only reinforce my belief in the value of journals in a legal assistant educational program:

> For my last journal entry, I thought I would assess this exercise. To tell you the truth, this exercise has been the hardest for me to keep up with. I have never been a good journal writer at any point in my life. As far as this assignment goes, it has been really helpful for me emotionally. I have used it to vent at times when I was frustrated about things that nobody cared to hear about.
>
> I also was able to use it to assess the things I learned throughout the semester. I liked being able to write without having to be so concerned with grammar or the analysis of an issue. It's been nice to just sit and write about my thoughts and concerns. I really feel this assignment has been beneficial for me especially this semester.
>
> I wish I could remember how therapeutic journal writing has been for me and continue to use it throughout my life. I feel this journal assignment has helped me to learn more about myself, and who I really am. Hopefully, I will be able to continue using a journal to communicate my thoughts and feelings in the future.

Each time I introduce the journal assignment to a new group of legal assistant students, I get moans and groans. But it has proven itself an effective, productive assignment on many levels. I can see it in the students' writing and I can read it in their entries. Although I had some concerns in the beginning about whether journals would work in such a technical and focused program as paralegal education, I believe that the writing helps to form the kind of people we need in law: people who are not only competent and careful, but also thoughtful, introspective, and balanced. Journal writing is clearly worth the students' time to do and my time to read and respond to.

Works Cited

Hurd, H. T. 1982. *Writing for Lawyers*. Pittsburgh: Journal Broadcasting & Communications.

13

Assessing Journals in the Disciplines
An Inductive Inquiry

Kathleen Blake Yancey, Ph.D., and Brian Huot, Ph.D.

It's a truism that when journals were initially introduced into classrooms in colleges and universities across the country, in the mid-1970s, they were understood as a safe "learning place" for students: that is, a place where students could take risks, could connect the personal with course material, could—as expressed in the defining expression of the time, one that continues today—*write to learn.* As such a place of exploration, journals were regularly *unevaluated:* They were understood to operate in what we might think of as a curricular assessment-free zone. Although "regular" course work, like tests and papers, might be assessed, journals were not—because of their personal nature, because of their special role in fostering learning, because of the presumed diminishing effect of assessing on the exploration we hoped to see in journals.

But as our title suggests, we think journals *should* be assessed—and perhaps more to the point, that *they already are assessed* routinely and informally, certainly, but also regularly and formally as well. If that's so—if journals already are assessed—and individual chapters in this book make that case very well, then the question isn't, "Should journals be assessed?"; the question is, "How should they be assessed?" This, we think, is a very good question: complex, revealing, interesting—one worthy of a journal entry itself.

To begin our entry, then, we'll define our major terms: *journal writing* and *assessment.* In our entry, we'll also talk about the roles that journals seem to play in different classes, observing that while many of those roles vary, in the aggregate there is a pattern here among the differences, a pattern that we could use to help us articulate our expectations. These expectations, we think, provide a basis for assessment—of both the formative and the summative variety.

Ultimately, our claim is that assessment has a key role to play in all learning, including the learning we see in journals.

The Value of Journal Writing

When journals were first used in the classroom, teachers weren't very clear about what journals could be, about what might be expected from them. Generally, faculty tended to see journals as a generic, general notebooklike place to learn, a place where both risk and the personal could be included.[1] Not surprisingly, when teachers read journals, they looked for (just about) anything and everything, working under two assumptions: (1) that students could easily have something to say that would enhance their leaning but that we faculty couldn't predict; and therefore, (2) that an open design for journals, which allowed the inclusion of whatever the student deemed relevant, provided best for the learning we couldn't predict. Consequently, what teachers often asked for was just about *anything* that the writer deemed relevant or interesting.

For journals in the disciplines, that thinking has changed. For one thing, the expression "writing-to-learn" has become *applied:* The learning that takes place in an engineering lecture is *discipline-based,* as is the learning taking place in a health professional class, but *they are discipline based differently.*[2] For another thing, as faculty have assigned, read, and thought about journals, they have refined how they conceive of them and how they use them. Put succinctly, they have particularized both forms of journals and purposes for them. In form, for instance:

- Sometimes journals are open letters between the instructor and the student.
- Sometimes they are individual journal entries that address assigned topics, what teachers call "directed writes."
- Sometimes they are individual e-mail exchanges, and sometimes the e-mail exchanges include an entire class.

The specific purposes of journals also vary. In Douglas E. Hirt's engineering lecture course, for instance, the purposes are three: (1) *to encourage active learning,* (2) *to encourage engagement with the material,* and (3) *to enable connections.* According to Hirt, "the goal of journal writing is to encourage students to be more active in the learning process. For this to be successful, the students must make an attempt to truly understand the material, and ask questions if something is not clear." Impressive questions, Hirt explains, often link students' knowledge from another discipline with the discipline under study, as in the question, "You said that Newtonian fluids do not support a normal stress. What about buoyancy?" Hirt appreciates this question, precisely because "the student took what he was learning in one course and related it to concepts learned in previous courses. . . . It is gratifying to see a large number of students relating the lecture material to material from other courses, to their everyday experiences, and to their industrial work experiences."

As important, the very act of raising questions itself teaches, Hirt argues. In the following example, for instance, he applauds the student for posing her own problem and then answering it, for, as he says, writing to learn, for thinking on the page. "I could follow the example you worked until you chose the velocity scale. I don't understand why you chose the maximum velocity. . . . Ah, yes, but the plot of v *vs.* x would be a little different, right? I think I answered my own question."

Another course, in a different discipline, enacts a different set of purposes for journals, one related to the course of study. In MaryEllen Vogt's teacher-education course, students work in the public schools as well as in their courses. Here, the journals focus on what MaryEllen Vogt calls *reflection,* which means that students are expected to review and thus learn from their work in the public schools. "We have found," she says, "that student teachers frequently use their e-journals to describe specific incidents that take place at school, ask questions about the incidents, wonder about how effectively they handled them, and reflect about what they have learned from the experience."

The journals provide a place for four related kinds of tasks: *describing, asking questions, wondering,* and *reflecting about what they have learned.* In working through this set of entries, Vogt says, students include the personal with the academic. Students record their "interactions with supervising teachers or students"; they reveal their "insecurities" and "self-doubt"; they include reflections about teaching as a career choice. This model of journal, then, invites students to work toward the general—toward thinking about professional issues—through the specifics of their practice elsewhere.

Still another model of journals is also oriented toward professional identity—in nursing, social work, and pharmacy—but it takes yet a different route to that goal. Sandra Balkema outlines three writing-to-learn purposes for students:

1. to articulate what they believe;
2. to consider what choices they might make (specialties, work environments, and lifestyles); and
3   to share their concerns with others.

In all these purposes, Balkema understands a specific relationship between a student's knowledge and his or her tendency to form opinions: "As they discover the extent and limits of their factual knowledge, they also begin to shape their opinions." Consequently, Balkema builds into the course an explicit preparation for the "what" that lies beyond the course: what she calls *continuing education.* "The flip side of the students' discovery of what they know is their recognizing the limits of their education and the need for continuing education. If they run into an article that they do not understand or do not like, I encourage them to analyze their reaction, to try to figure out why they had difficulty." Balkema also builds into this model of journal an evaluation that is itself a cumulative activity:

> At the end of the semester . . . I ask them to evaluate the journal writing assignment by identifying the [professional] journal they found most valuable and what they found most beneficial about the assignment. I ask them to identify the criteria they use (or plan to use) when subscribing to a journal: the cost, an affiliation with professional organization, a focus on research, a focus on practice, a mixture of research and practice, or what?

Bobbie Othmer and Terry Scott describe a fourth model of journal, this one used in a computer science class. This model is grounded in five assumptions.

- Journals encourage learning course content.
- Journals promote problem solving.
- Journals help students keep current in their field.
- Journals provide opportunities for reflection on ethics.
- Journals promote writing fluency.

Even within one of these assumptions, the purposes are many.

> Students learn the subject matter as well as how to think about it. Writing in a journal provides an opportunity for students to make connections between new knowledge and their prior knowledge and experience, to make new knowledge personal, and to reflect on processes, meaning, and experience. This kind of writing involves the student in both active and deep processes of learning and critical thinking. Without this kind of questioning and responding, information from the instructor and texts may be stored away undigested and unprocessed and thus not in a form that can be retrieved and applied in appropriate situations.

Because the journal plays such an important intellectual role in the class, it plays a large curricular role as well. Students write nearly every day, and "writing should allow for continuity between entries, which is important for the class and the journal." This model of journal, then, is both central and integral to the class—a primary place of intellectual work, a place where intellectual work takes various forms.

Similarities in Varied Journals

While these models of journals vary, they also are alike—if only because they operate in the same "rhetorical situation," that of a particular kind of class where

- the student is assumed to be an active participant;
- the material of the class is assumed to be related to material beyond the class: to concepts from other classes, from other educational settings, from other work-related settings, from settings the student has yet to encounter;

- one role of the student is to find and articulate these connections;
- the journal provides a place for such articulations; and
- through such articulations students *become.*

Put differently, what these journals all do is ask the student to undertake a central goal: to *develop the identity of an active, critical learner.* To develop this identity, the student thinks in explicit ways:

- *think as person,* which enables consideration of connections as well as ethics;
- *think as student developing knowledge in a particular field,* which requires that questions be raised and that disciplinary problems be solved;
- *think as student with other knowledge,* developing knowledge in a particular field so that there is a kind of comparison, contrast, and (possible) synthesis;
- *think as reflective student,* reviewing past practice, weighing alternatives, making judgments and solving problems, and projecting into the future.

As important, students who engage in these kinds of thinking are engaged in very multiple ways: they

- are engaged with the intellectual material of the course so that they *ask about it and know it;*
- are engaged with the intellectual material of the course so that they *understand* it, can *relativize* it, and can *reflect* upon it;
- are engaged with others in making meaning, so that their *meaning-making is both individual and social.*

The Value of Assessment

So how do we assess the work in identity formation, the work in thinking, that we see in journals? And what do we mean by assessment? And, not unrelated, should we assess at all?

Sometimes it's easier to define what we don't mean. What we don't mean by assessment is providing grades, although sometimes faculty do grade as one means of assessment. What we also don't mean is evaluating in the sense of finding right and wrong. What we *do* mean by assessment is enacted by two questions: (1) What do we value in student work? and (2) How can we communicate what we value to students so as to enhance their learning? In other words, at its best, assessment is itself about inquiry, about learning. And in general, these questions have taken two forms: formative assessment and summative assessment. In the classroom, formative assessment is the review of student work in order to help the student; it includes practices like reading and responding to student work so as to enhance learning. Summative assessment is the review of work in order to draw a final conclusion; it includes grades.

But before we move to specific formative and summative strategies, we might consider the obvious: Why assess in the first place? Five good reasons come to mind quickly.

Assessment is ubiquitous; it happens all the time.   Even when faculty don't include a formal assessment of student journals, they know what they like and thus want to see. (Again, the pages of this volume make this point cogently.) In other words, a review—reading and judgment—about the value of the journals already takes place. Including it formally simply makes visible to the students what is currently and too often hidden from them.

Students need to know teacher values.   Assessment can make what is invisible explicit and thus formative. If we know what we value in student learning, and the discussion in this text as well as elsewhere indicates we do, we owe it to our students to tell them what those values are. When we don't tell students what we value, we deny them the chance to develop along clearly demarcated channels, or even to resist in an informed way. Rather, students feel that they are shooting blind at a moving target.

Journals count, too.   If what we value is important, then we do well to include journals or a journal entry as one of the many kinds of texts we assess. There is a saying in assessment circles that it's not what you expect, it's what you inspect that counts, that is. Linking journals and assessment makes the learning that takes place in journals count.

Assessment makes our expectations clear.   When faculty include assessment, they articulate their own expectations. This itself is a learning experience; such articulation stipulates a contract for learning between teacher and students.

Faculty learn from their own assessments.   When faculty have their expectations articulated and shared with the students, they have a basis for reviewing and enhancing their own work. They can see where their articulations fall short, where students exceed those expectations, where expectations are badly phrased or misapplied. In other words, a kind of learning about our own teaching is also made possible by *this kind of assessment.*

The idea of *this kind of assessment* is crucial here since some classic assessment strategies that don't foster the kind of learning we've been talking about are often applied to journals. For instance, there is the "count 'em" strategy: number of pages, number of entries, number of words per entry. There is also the count/no count method: full credit for doing "enough," as defined earlier; no credit for anything else. This isn't the kind of assessment we are advocating, of course. To provide guidelines—for instance, that learning-rich journals typically require a certain number of pages, consider certain kinds of questions—is helpful. But guidelines aren't assessments.

One last question before we talk about some specific strategies: Will linking assessment and journals change the nature of the engagement? Yes, we think so. But if the assessment is worth having—if it is substantial and shapes behavior *so that thinking and engagement are highlighted*—then it's a change we'll want.

Formative Assessment Strategies

What can formative assessment contribute to the learning we see in journals? It can help us see the relationship between and among (1) what we ask for, (2) what we expect, and (3) how we respond.

What we ask for matters. As we've seen, models of journals vary, and given their different purposes, this variation is appropriate. In fact, given what we know about the disciplinarity of knowledge formation, we might say that such variation is itself to be expected. But what happens is that as students move from one class to another, the very word *journal* changes; it means something different from one setting to the next, even within a major. So an instructor's first task is to define what *journal* means in that specific setting. A second, related task is to consider how the instructor and students will know if the journal is working: that is, a given task is assumed to produce a certain effect. What is the task, then? And what is the expected effect? When these specifics are outlined, several benefits accrue: (1) the role of the journal is defined; (2) what is expected is clarified—so that the blind moving target takes on a location, shape, and color; (3) the grounds for a response are provided. In sum, the kind of journal—comprehensive, reflective, question-based, continuous—becomes a starting place for specific modes of assessment.

A journal is completed; it takes on a reader (us). How do we respond? The literature on response to formal papers is pretty clear: Tell 'em what you like and tell 'em how to revise (see, for instance, Sommers 1980; Light 1991; Smith 1997). But that literature on response is intended to improve writing specifically, whereas our brief survey of journals (above) suggests that what is valued isn't writing as performance so much (the kind we see in research papers, for example), but rather two rhetorical moves: (1) *thinking on the page* and (2) *writing as engagement*. If this analysis is correct, then our response would be in kind: We engage with the issues as well. We too, in other words, think on the page in *reply* to the students (Yancey 1998). We continue the dialogue not only because modeling what we want can be very helpful to students, but also *because we too find the issues engaging;* that is, there is real intellectual engagement. When it works, then, writing to engage engages not only the student writer, but also the faculty reader, who becomes a writer-in-reply. The journal is a place of engagement, of real discussion, where claim and reply, reply to reply, and so on become *the stuff of the journal.*

A second role for the formative assessment of response is to show students what's working—and what therefore is "likable" in their work. Both Peter Elbow (1993) and Donald Daiker (1989) make the point that in our obsession with critiquing what's not working—which is the form that response to text often takes—too often we don't let students know what *is* working. In the case of journals, of course, the point isn't so much to let students know what works in their writing per se as it is to let them know what is valuable in their thinking. Do we see, for instance, connections between our classes and what they have learned elsewhere? Do we see students sorting out from their own learning what is most important? As responders to student journals, then, we have two rhetorical moves that we need to make. First, we need to identify what is likable in students' journals (Yancey 1998), since once students identify their own work as likable, they are more inclined to repeat it, to extend it, and to move beyond it.[3] Second, in identifying what's likable, we need to use *a language of response*—using words like synthesize, connect, *relativize,* and so on—that students can begin to use in talking about, and thus enhancing, their own thinking processes.

Summative Assessment Strategies

Ultimately, of course, there is the summative assessment that we might also make; it's called for every time the grade roster shows up in our mailboxes and we need to assign a grade to each student. Here, too, there are many possibilities.

Pass/Fail

Sometimes, we can simply assign a pass/fail grade to a journal, based on the criteria shared with students at the beginning of the class that were defined and exemplified for them in their own work by careful response. The key item in this model of summative assessment, of course, is the careful response. It is that response to a specific text that gives color and shape to abstract expectations and criteria. Without color and shape, there is no context for the grade.

Self-Assessment

Other times, we can include a self-assessment component, perhaps like the "extension" described earlier in this book by Sandra Balkema, one that *confirms* our earlier impressions of the journal. Alternatively, we might ask students for a cumulative reading of their own work, a review assessment in which they determine what the most critical learning was, for them, and why: This is a different kind of confirmation. Regardless of the specific type, confirmation is useful for both student and teacher, for student since it provides one more opportunity to learn, for teacher since it provides one more occasion to make a judgment, and sound judgments tend to rely on multiple opportunities. (Grades of course are the ultimate semester judgment.) As important, self-assessment suggests to students that their journal work is valuable in yet another way: They can revise their thinking at the term's end, a thinking that improved in specified ways over the term—as indicated by criteria.

Portfolios

It might be that for a summative assessment, journals contribute to a portfolio of work, one composed entirely of a specified number of journals (Gold 1992), or one that includes several components (e.g., a midterm, formal papers, and journal entries), of which journals are only a part (for a model of this kind of portfolio, see Allen et al. 1997). Here, all the journals count for learning, and some are selected for summative assessment. If this option is chosen, a reflective text will be useful as well—to indicate why the specific entries were chosen, what they demonstrate, and so on.[4]

In three of these cases, the summative assessment itself has formative value: that is, it provides another opportunity to learn—and to learn that which has not been learned previously, to extend what has been learned. Which is the best that assessment can offer.

A Final Comment on Assessment

As we have noted elsewhere, many faculty are uncomfortable with assessment—and for good reasons if we think of assessment as dichotomous (e.g., right/wrong), as late-in-the-game (e.g., grades), as in opposition to learning. Assessment, however, isn't synonymous with grades; as we've indicated, it can operate entirely without grades. Nor is it in opposition to learning: quite the contrary. What it needs to operate well is a clear focus: on students learning in a specific context about specific material and making of that material what they can—with our help.

To the extent that assessment helps us do this, it helps us all, especially those of us who use journals.

Notes

1. It could well be that conventional wisdom about the evaluating of journals got stalled on the issue of the personal in journals: Faculty were understandably reluctant to evaluate the personal, in much the same way that faculty often hesitate to assess poetry, i.e., because of its personal quality.

2. For a fuller discussion of this point, see Bazerman.

3. In some ways this is a surprisingly provocative claim, given some understandings of what motivates students. In a recent and well-publicized *Harper's* article on students today, for example, the author—a faculty member at the University of Virginia—claims that in order to learn, students have to accept that *disliking* something about themselves is required. Our review of the attitudes expressed in this volume, as well as our own experience, suggests that this view is wrongheaded, and probably counterproductive, a point made eloquently by one of the author's own students in her reply to the article, which appeared in a later issue of the magazine. See the September 1997 issue of *Harper's*.

4. For a discussion of the kinds of reflective texts faculty might want to consider, see Yancey, *Reflection in the Writing Classroom*, particularly Chapter Four.

Works Cited

Allen, M., W. Condon, M. Dickson, C. Forbes, G. Meece, and K. Yancey. 1997. "Portfolios, WAC, Email and Assessment: An Inquiry on Portnet." In *Situating Portfolios: Four Perspectives,* ed. K. B. Yancey and I. Weiser, 370–84. Logan, Utah: Utah State University Press.

Bazerman, C. 1985. *The Informed Writer: Using Sources in the Disciplines,* 2nd ed. Boston: Houghton Mifflin.

Daiker, D. 1989. "Learning to Praise." In *Writing and Response: Theory, Practice, and Research,* ed. C. Anson, 103–14. Urbana, Illinois: National Council of Teachers of English.

Elbow, P. 1993. "Ranking, Sorting, Liking: Sorting Out Three Forms of Judgment." *College English* 55: 187–206.

Gold, S. E. 1992. "Increasing Student Autonomy Through Portfolios." In *Portfolios in the Writing Classroom: An Introduction,* ed. K. B. Yancey, 103–14. Urbana, Illinois: National Council of Teachers of English.

Light, R. 1991. *The Harvard Assessment Seminars: Second Report.* Cambridge: Harvard University Graduate School of Education and Kennedy School of Government.

Sommers, N. 1980. "Revision Strategies of Student Writers and Adult Experienced Writers." *College Composition and Communication* 31: 378–88.

Smith, S. 1997. "The Genre of the End Comment." *College Composition and Communication* 48: 249–69.

Yancey, K. B. 1998. *Reflection in the Writing Classroom.* Logan, Utah: Utah State University Press.

Afterword

When Journals Don't Work

Toby Fulwiler, Ph.D.

As much as I believe in the pedagogical power of journals to help students and teachers advance writing and learning, I also know they don't work every time, nor in every setting, nor for everyone. Sometimes, instructors who value journals for themselves are unable to convince students of their value. Other times, instructors who have assigned journals effectively in the past find journals failing in the present. Still other times, instructors who find journals effective in one course find them ineffective in another. Meanwhile, some people who resolve to keep journals simply fail to keep at it, finding them more bothersome than profitable.

This final chapter examines the circumstances under which journals fail as a teaching or learning strategy and offers possible remedies to overcome those failures. Following are some of the difficulties I've heard expressed by faculty who have assigned journals to college students.

My subject is technical and not suited to journal writing.   That may be true, but only if what you teach is cut-and-dried (as the students say), lends itself to rote memory, and is a matter of fact, right and wrong, or black-and-white. However, if your subject is technical (math, engineering, economics, chemistry), but also open to discussion, speculation, exploration, and doubt, it's not true. Odds are that exploring the subjective and debatable areas of technical education through journal writing will increase, not decrease, student interest in your subject.

I can't see myself saying the words, "Take out your journals."   Don't. Here are three cautions about assigning journals in the first place: (1) If you never have kept a journal yourself, if you aren't going to keep one with your students, or if you personally don't believe in the idea, don't assign journals to your students; you need to both believe in them and know how they work in practice to make them work well as assignments. (2) If you don't like reading personal pronouns, sloppy language, awkward handwriting, or unfinished thought, don't collect student journals, for nearly all honest journals contain a great deal of such language. And (3) if you want to maintain a strictly academic relationship with your students and not catch their personal habits, values, biases, and beliefs, don't read student journals, for such entries commonly appear in journals.

When I announce to a class that I require journals, I hear an audible groan. Unfortunately, I've heard that too, and I think I know why. On my syllabus I've written the word *journals* and in class I say the word *journals,* but I'm afraid what the students hear, instead, is the word *diary.* They expect to be required to share their personal lives with instructors they hardly know—an impression they've picked up from journal assignments somewhere else in their previous school experience. There are two ways I counter this: First, I explain that an academic journal is written from a personal point of view, yes, but about the subject matter of the course, not about their private lives. Second, I explain that sharing entries is voluntary. And there's another way, as well, to head off this groan: Don't call them journals; instead, call them "logs" or "learning logs" or "notebooks" or "field notebooks" or "workbooks" or "day books" or "commonplace books."

Students are writing all their entries the night before I collect them. I know, I once spent a weekend at our family cottage with my undergraduate daughter who was doing just that for an English course—composing a month's worth of journal entries because the journal was to be collected Monday. That used to happen to me, too, when I assigned journals but then put them on the back burner and kept them there until midterm when I asked to see them. All that changed when I moved the journal assignment to the front burner, used them daily in class, and students saw their utility and value. Here's what to do: Ask students to write in journals daily—or at least weekly—in class, for five to ten minutes, at the beginning of class. Then follow up by sharing a passage with a neighbor or listening to everyone read a line out loud or basing a small-group discussion on what group members wrote. At the end of five weeks, every student will have ten to fifteen entries from class alone, so faking won't be necessary.

A comment on faking it. It used to anger me to imagine a student writing several weeks worth of entries on a set of assignments at one sitting, the night before the journal was due, twelve different pens and pencils to suggest different composing times. However, I changed my mind after watching my daughter spend hours and hours fabricating journal entries to look as if they'd been religiously written daily during the course. She reread chapters, looked up passages, copied in quotes, invented questions, created connections, speculated and wondered, arranging each entry in a plausible chronological order.

Fabricating that journal in one weekend was, in fact, a heroic act of composing, worth the full credit she no doubt earned. Her role in class discussion was probably less than it could have been, but the writing, bunched up though it was, did its usual magic.

Students complain that journal writing every class period is boring.   And perhaps it is. The trick here is to present thoughtful and perhaps surprising prompts for students to write about each week so that the writing never becomes predictable. I want it to be predictable that they will write, but what they write about I want to be surprising. If I'm always asking for "one insight about the readings" or "what did you learn in class today," after a few weeks it becomes predictable. So even though I think those are good questions, I try to invent new ones week to week to keep them a bit off balance. (*What* is he going to ask us to write about this week?) In fact, my best prompts come from reviewing the past class and anticipating the next, figuring out what I need do most to keep on learning.

My students claim to be journaled out.   Students are sometimes required to keep journals in several classes at the same time, especially in schools with strong Writing-Across-the-Curriculum programs. If that's the case, they may report weariness at being asked to keep yet another journal—so now they've got one each in poly sci, soc, and English. I've heard this, too, since I've promoted journals in faculty writing workshops across the University of Vermont curriculum for better than a decade. First, of course, if you know other faculty are assigning journals, suggest that students keep their separate journals within one loose-leaf binder with dividers for each course—that way they carry around only one notebook and hand in selections as requested and still keep on writing. But the only action that will really stop the complaint is to make sure the journal assignments in your class are highly purposeful, and that the purpose is evident to your students. The best way to demonstrate purpose is to provide challenging journal-writing prompts each week in class, and to use that writing to advance both class discussion and formal writing projects. Students who recognize that journal writing makes class more interesting simply stop complaining.

When I read the journals, all I find are safe and superficial entries.   Dull journal writing can happen anytime and be done by anyone—I've done my share in the past and am likely to do more in the future. But other times, I write more lively and interesting entries. However, if what you read in sample student journal entries is primarily dull, teacher-pleasing prose, your students are either bored with your course (big problem, not one I can solve), they don't trust you, or they don't know what lively journal writing can look like. Assuming the problem is caution and ignorance rather than boredom, the best solution is to share lively samples of student journal writing with the class by reading them aloud or showing them (in the student's own handwriting) on an overhead projector. Once students see that you value a range of journal voices, from sassy and irreverent to serious and searching, well, you'll get more interesting writing from then on.

If I stop using them in class, students stop writing in them.   I've done this more than once, used journals well for a few weeks, by working them hard in class, but then, for one reason or another, stopped attending to them. After a lull of a few weeks, it becomes hard to say "Take out your journals." To prevent this, announce in class or write in your syllabus—preferably both—that you intend to start every class (or every Friday class, for example) with five or ten minutes of journal writing. It's a public declaration that this is important writing and you're willing to bind yourself to the practice. It's not foolproof, but if you establish the habit, both you and your students will look forward to the daily or weekly writing time.

I assigned journals in three classes, but collecting and reading them nearly killed me.   If you're going to collect journals from several classes or a large class, stagger your collecting, so you don't have to read them all the same week. In any case, I'd recommend collecting selected or edited pages from journals, so you don't need a box to carry the journals to and from classes. In other words, ask students to keep their journals in loose-leaf notebooks, and ask for a selection of five to ten pages periodically. That way, students tend to give you the wheat not the chaff, and you spend *less* time reading *more* interesting entries. Or, if you write in them daily and share them in class, don't collect them at all—they've done their work. The main drawback here is that you miss out on reading interesting student voices—especially those of the quieter members of your class.

If I don't grade journals, students won't treat them seriously.   It's true that students hate busywork that doesn't, somehow, count. The trick here is to count journals quantitatively, but to avoid the trap of grading them qualitatively, like quizzes. As soon as you start grading journal entries on the correctness of their insights, you shut down a writer's willingness to take risks with ideas; what you find, instead, is sure, safe, and routine. When journals become the repository for sure, safe, and routine ideas, students don't want to write them and I don't want to read them. In contrast, I love to read journal writing that explores or speculates or wonders or doubts—and students find journal writing more interesting when they feel the freedom to write that way. In fact, my own experience tells me that writing about what I don't already understand leads to more complete understanding—the writing will either lead me there itself or reveal the gaps I now need to fill in. My recommendation? Count entries or pages or weigh by the pound or give points for physical evidence, but let journals be one place in the academic world where they can write and be wrong and not get clobbered for it.

If I don't grade them, how do I respond to them?   Though you may have assigned them, serious journals always remain the writer's personal territory, not yours. Let the journal writer's voice be what it may. This is not the place to comment on matters of grammar, punctuation, spelling, or style, for when writers catch fast impromptu thoughts, they don't necessarily write carefully. (If you want careful writing, assign formal papers and make sure the writers have a chance to revise and edit.) To respond to journals, use your letter-writing voice, addressing each student by name, respectfully, showing that you appreciate the opportunity to browse in his or her thought. Raise questions or suggest other directions, but do so in a helpful, not a corrective, voice. Sign your name.

Every time I collect and read student journals, I feel as if I'm prying. Even when I ask to see only self-selected journal entries, I feel as if I'm trespassing on students' private turf. In truth, serious journal entries are written for a writer's self—if they are not, they really are not journals as I understand them. My best solution to this, in recent years, is to assign journals, but to collect letters. I ask students to write a letter to me once a week and to draw on their journal entries for material. While they could simply recopy journal entries to share with me, most students find letter writing an opportunity to more completely finish or communicate a thought started in a journal entry. I collect and read these letters, and I deliver a letter back the next class period—one to the whole class (Dear Classmates) in which I quote their various concerns and address them in a friendly voice. This way, students continue to write informally and honestly, but know from the git-go they are addressing me. Now, when they share informal thoughts with me in letters, they do so intentionally. And because student letters to me are intentional, they are deeper, richer, and more focused in my direction than journal entries ever were, though they are perhaps more guarded as well.

What about electronic journals, do they work?   The advent of e-mail and access to the Internet has opened up all kinds of new possibilities for informal writing. Instead of browsing through student journals or asking students to write paper letters to me, I have used e-mail exchanges instead, and this is what I've found: E-mail is an ideal medium for short timely communiqués between instructor and student about specific questions related to course and assignments, and in this sense e-mail substitutes well for short conferences otherwise held after class, during office hours, or via telephone. At the same time, perhaps because of the speed with which it operates or the conventions to which we've all become accustomed, I've found e-mail to be a less reflective medium than either journal or letter writing. In journals students clearly write to themselves, whereas e-mail implies an audience. In e-mail letters to me, in place of printed-out paper letters, students write more briefly and more carelessly—I infer that they write faster and take less considered time with e-mail composing. Finally, if you do want to take advantage of the out-of-class dialogical potential of e-mail to encourage informal discussions of class assignments, I have three suggestions: (1) require a certain number of exchanges (student-student or student-instructor) a week—though required, the students usually enjoy such truly interesting work; (2) develop some means to witness that these exchanges occur (e.g., ask for sample exchanges to be copied to you or printed out in a portfolio); and (3) count such exchanges quantitatively as you would journal or letter assignments.

Let's face it, journals (or letters or e-mail messages) are no different from any other fairly good assignment you make: The first time you assign it, you find out what works and what doesn't. The next time, learning by experience, it works better. Next time, better still. But after that, be careful, because if it becomes too predictable for you, it'll start getting worse again. Since I believe absolutely in the value of writing as a mode of learning, my own best solution is to vary genres, formats, frequency, and media. Emphasize journals one year, letters the next, e-mail the next, and so on. Keep good records, examine the results, and next time, try something else.

Appendix

Setting Up Successful Journals
Practical Tips
Susan Gardner, Ph.D.

When as a teacher you decide to use a journal (or field notebook or learning log of some kind) in a course, you'll need to make many decisions. Successful assignments take careful preparation. What follows is a checklist of areas to consider as you create your journal assignment.

- ❏ Think about the goals of the course first. Ask yourself, "What do I want my students to get out of doing this kind of writing assignment?"

- ❏ Decide on the purposes for the journal assignment itself, e.g., improve writing fluency, respond to reading, connect lab activities to other knowledge, solve problems, and so on.

- ❏ Write out your instructions and purposes for the assignment so that students will have something concrete to refer to.

- ❏ As you prepare the assignment, think through the following areas and include them in your written description as needed:

  - ➜ List explicit goals for or purposes of the assignment.
  - ➜ Indicate format conventions, including:
    - What the journal will physically look like or materials to be used.

      Examples: loose-leaf notebook
      spiral or bound notebook
      e-mail messages
      on computer disk, audio cassette, or videotape
      pen, pencil, word processed
      one or both sides of pages
      use of tape or staples for additional materials

174

- How the journal will be sequenced, i.e., the organization.

    Examples: table of contents
    page numbering
    dates
    titles
    by topic, assignment, or chronology
    by location or context

→ Describe type and style of writing allowed or preferred.

- Types can include such things as narration, description, summary, informal essay, letter, drawing, personal reflection, free writing, problem solving, and so on.

- Levels of language and sentence structure to be used.

    Examples: personal language
    scientific, objective language
    stream-of-consciousness
    informal, colloquial language
    personal code
    whole sentences or lists and fragments

- Whether or not you mark grammar, punctuation, and spelling errors.

→ Explain accommodations made for disabled students, e.g., taping rather than writing entries, dictating entries to someone who writes or word processes entries, and so forth.

→ Indicate the content you expect—what students should write about or are free to write about.

- Explain how topics are to be generated for this assignment.

    Example: unfocused, student-selected—whatever comes
    to mind
    focused, student-selected—in answer to a question
    but with latitude to select approach, order, and
    actual content
    focused, teacher-selected—students asked to write
    on same topic or list of topics

- Describe, if appropriate to the assignment, how illustrations, drawings, sketches, photos, clippings, artifacts, and so on are to be integrated into the journal.

- Determine how topics of a personal nature are to be handled—who reads, issues of privacy, acceptable content.

- Clearly define right to privacy for all students in class.

- Explain your legal responsibility to report certain kinds of material if written in the journal.

- Decide how, if any, reading assignments, problem solving, and so on will be integrated into the journal.

→ Identify the audience, or who is going to see or read the journal entries.

Possible audiences: writer only (the self)
                      writer plus the teacher
                      writer plus a selected classmate
                      writer plus the teacher plus classmates

→ Describe the length of entries—either in number of pages or amount of time spent writing.

→ Describe the frequency of entries, or how often students are required to write in the journal.

→ Indicate the total quantity of entries, or an actual target number of pages students need to write to complete the assignment.

→ Detail the time for writing entries, or if all writing is inside of class time, outside of class time, or a combination of both.

→ Indicate the due dates, or when the journals will be collected, plus a clear explanation of penalties for not having the assignment ready on the due date.

→ Indicate what type of response students can expect to the journals.

→ Describe what use will be made of journals—no obvious use except to fulfill a requirement, use before class discussions, examples taken from journals, integration with other assignments, and so on.

→ Detail what grading or evaluation criteria will be used for the journal assignment.

Answer the following questions.

- Will the journal be graded?

- If graded, will it be graded on quantity of pages, quality of insights, recording of data, and so on?

- If not graded, will it be given credit of some sort toward the overall course grade?

→ Describe how the journal figures into the overall course grade.

→ Explain how and when students can expect the return of their journals.

→ List any other specifications, expectations, or idiosyncrasies of the journal assignment or for you personally.

❏ Think about having students do something with their journal at the end of the term.

> Example: Students review their entries, create a table of contents, and write a final summary of their journal that synthesizes their growth or learning over the course of keeping the journal.

❏ After you've finished writing the journal assignment, review the list of suggestions in these pages, and then answer the following questions for yourself:

1. Have you created a journal assignment that is an integral rather than an added-on part of the course?

2. Have you as the teacher committed to using the journal during class in some way?

3. Have you as the teacher committed to making individual comments or providing responses on a number of the journal entries?

4. Have you picked out specific points in the course where journals will be collected and responded to so that students don't fall into procrastination about writing entries?

5. What plans have you made for students to reread, review, or reflect on their journal entries occasionally throughout the course?

6. What specifically will students do at the end of the assignment so that they benefit from the synthesis of their learning, progress, or thinking on a subject?

Selected Bibliography

The resources listed and briefly annotated below have been selected because they are either an entire book about journals, or in some portion they treat journals seriously as a tool for writing and learning.

Anson, C. M. & R. Beach. 1995. *Journals in the Classroom: Writing to Learn.* Norwood, MA: Christopher-Gordon Publishers, Inc. Comprehensive discussion of using journals as a central method of teaching and for improving student learning. This book describes the multifaceted purposes, uses, and forms journals take. It also provides strategies and ideas for using journals with secondary and college students. The collection does not feature journals across the curriculum extensively, but it does include an excellent description of published journals and how to respond and evaluate journal writing.

Bean, J. C. 1996. *Engaging Ideas: The Professor's Guide to Integrating Writing, Critical Thinking, and Active Learning in the Classroom.* San Francisco: Jossey-Bass. In a chapter on informal, exploratory writing activities, Bean suggests many uses for journals, double-entry notebooks, reading logs, and so forth across the disciplines. His pedagogical descriptions include clear guidelines for setting up the assignments, knowing how to respond and evaluate these writing-to-learn activities, and how to actively integrate this type of writing into classes.

Burnham, C. 1994. "Journals." In *Blair Resources for Teaching Writing,* 1–28. Englewood Cliffs, NJ: Prentice-Hall. A short pamphlet used as supplementary material to *The Blair Handbook,* Burnham's "Journals" succinctly describes journal assignments used for both personal and academic purposes. It dispels some of the myths of journal writing as all freewriting yet shows how exploratory journal writing moves students into deeper learning. "Journals" also describes how academic logs can be used to document learning through structured reading responses contained in a kind of writer's notebook or commonplace book.

Fulwiler, T., ed, 1987. *The Journal Book.* Portsmouth, NH: Boynton/Cook Publishers. Forty-two chapters by teachers and instructors in different disciplines and at different grade levels, kindergarten through college. Each chapter describes the use of journals as an aid to teaching. Many provide authentic samples of journal writing as well as suggestions for using them in class and assessing the results.

Fulwiler, T. & A. Young, eds. 1986. *Writing Across the Disciplines: Research into Practice.* Portsmouth, NH: Boynton/Cook Publishers. This collection describes the impact of the WAC movement at one institution, Michigan Tech, and is a valuable professional resource in itself. Two chapters, however, "Writing to Learn: Engineering Student Journals" and "Journal Writing in Mathematics" are particularly helpful for their insights into the uses of journals in more technical or professional areas.

————. 1982. *Language Connections: Writing and Reading Across the Curriculum.*
Urbana: NCTE. An early collection of Writing-Across-the-Curriculum essays that
provides helpful descriptions and pedagogical strategies for using writing as a tool
for learning. Especially significant is Fulwiler's chapter "The Personal Connection:
Journal Writing Across the Curriculum." Actual examples from a number of disciplines show how both personal and academic writing can be fostered in one type
of assignment, the journal.

Howard, R. M. & S. Jamieson. 1995. *The Bedford Guide to Teaching Writing in the Disciplines: An Instructor's Desk Reference.* Boston: St. Martin's Press. Although this
book describes a self-contained course in teaching writing in the disciplines, the
authors see it primarily as a handy reference tool. It is very practical, filled with
teaching ideas and strategies, and grounded in Writing-Across-the-Curriculum theory and research. It contains a superb chapter on assigning and evaluating academic
journals.

Poirrier, G. P. 1997. *Writing-to-Learn: Curricular Strategies for Nursing and Other
Disciplines.* New York: NLN Press. A book dedicated to writing-to-learn, the heart
of the WAC movement, is a solid resource for teachers in professional and technical disciplines. The chapter on using journals with nursing students features extensive student samples and describes the many benefits of journal writing in a
clinical program.

Soven, M. K. 1996. *Write to Learn: A Guide to Writing Across the Curriculum.* Cincin-
nati: South-Western College Publishing. A slim volume that concisely describes
how to incorporate more writing into any discipline and offers nuts-and-bolts suggestions on everything from creating assignments to responding to or evaluating
student products. The section on journal writing includes model assignments from
courses in criminal justice, finance, and Spanish.

Stillman, P. 1984. *Writing Your Way.* Portsmouth, NH: Boynton/Cook Publishers. An
unorthodox text on writing that can be used for secondary or freshman-level composition courses, Stillman's book has one of the best discussions ever written of
what journals are and are not. "Of Myself, for Myself" explores audience, topic
choice, personal connections, academic uses, and so on of journal writing. The
chapter provides excellent background for teachers wanting to implement journals
in their courses.

Contributors

Janet Ashbury is a family physician and lecturer in the Department of Family Medicine at Queen's University in Kingston, Ontario, Canada. She has taught medical students for several of the last fourteen years in the clinical and communication skills program at Queen's, taking a large portion of time out from teaching and family medicine to be at home with her three children. Janet's e-mail address is ashburyt@post.queensu.ca

Sandra Balkema is Professor of English in the Department of Languages and Literature at Ferris State University in Big Rapids, Michigan. Sandy also serves as the Coordinator of the Technical and Professional Communication B.S. Program at Ferris. In addition to teaching a variety of writing courses, Sandy has been an editor of course and study guides, a technical trainer, writer and designer of brochures, grant writer, and judge for technical communication competitions. Sandy's e-mail address is balkemas@ferris.edu

Richard Birtwhistle is a family physician and a professor in the Departments of Family Medicine and Community Health and Epidemiology at Queen's University in Kingston, Ontario, Canada. He was director of Clinical Skills for the Faculty of Medicine at Queen's University for several years during which time he helped develop the first-year communication skills course. He is currently the Associate Dean of Undergraduate Medical Education.

Beth Daniell is an Associate Professor of English at Clemson University in South Carolina. Her Ph.D. is from the University of Texas at Austin. She has published on literacy, orality, and composition theory in a number of journals and collections and she frequently presents papers at the Conference on College Composition and Communication. She is currently writing a book about the intersections of literacy and spirituality. Beth's e-mail address is dbeth@clemson.edu

Jane Danielewicz, an Assistant Professor at University of North Carolina, Chapel Hill, holds a joint appointment in the Department of English and the School of Education. She has published essays on the theory and practice of composition; a recent essay in *Dialogue* explores the influence that writing groups may have on the nature and presence of voice in college writers. Her research interests include the evolution, acquisition, and uses of print and technological literacy; composition pedagogy; discourse theory and analysis; and teacher education (secondary and postsecondary levels). Jane's e-mail address is janedan@email.unc.edu

Ann Dobie is Professor of English at the University of Southwestern Louisiana where she directs graduate studies in rhetoric and the University's Writing-Across-the-Curriculum Program. She has published numerous articles about the teaching of writing and several textbooks, including *Comprehension and Composition: An Introduction* *to the Essay.* Her latest book is *Something in Common: Contemporary Louisiana Stories.* She is State Coordinator for the Louisiana Writing Projects and a member of the Task Force of the National Writing Project. Currently she is serving as Co-Director of Writing for the Challenge, a grant from the Annenberg Foundation to improve the teaching of writing in rural schools. Ann's e-mail address is dobie@usl.edu

Gary Dohrer is Associate Professor of English at Weber State University where he is director of the Writing-Across-the-Curriculum Program. He also teaches English methods classes and Children's and Young Adult Literature. He is deeply involved with the use of technology to assist writing in the disciplines and instilling this use of technology into secondary instruction of English. He lives in a log home in the mountains outside of Ogden, Utah, with his wife Kim, a high school principal, and their two dogs. Gary's e-mail address is gdohrer@weber.edu

Barbara Fletcher is the Director of the Clinical Learning Centre (CLC) at Queen's University in Kingston, Ontario, Canada. The CLC is a site for experiential education activities for the faculties of Medicine, Nursing, and Rehabilitation Therapy. Barbara's academic interests include socialization in the professions, self-reflection, and journal writing in experiential learning. She helped develop the first-year medicine communication skills course at Queen's. Barbara's e-mail address is fletcheb@post.queensu.ca

Toby Fulwiler has directed the writing program at the University of Vermont since 1983. Before that he taught at Michigan Tech and the University of Wisconsin where, in 1973, he also received his Ph.D. in American Literature. At Vermont he teaches introductory and advanced writing classes. Recent books include *College Writing* (2nd edition, 1997); *When Writing Teachers Teach Literature,* co-edited with Art Young (1996); and *The Blair Handbook,* co-authored with Alan Hayakawa (2nd edition, 1997). He also edited *The Journal Book* (1987) which proved to be the seedbed for this project. Toby's e-mail address is t-fulwile@moose.uvm.edu

Susan Gardner is currently the Writing Coordinator for the Faculty at Westminster College of Salt Lake City. Formerly a high school English teacher and director of a college writing program, Susan earned her Ph.D. in English and Education at The University of Michigan. At Westminster she *is* the WAC program. She presents workshops for faculty on effective teaching, active learning, critical thinking, and writing on her own campus and at other colleges. For the past fifteen summers, she has conducted workshops with varied emphases (writing theory, integrating writing and literature, writing and science, computers and writing) for elementary and secondary teachers, principals, and superintendents. Susan has used journals extensively in her teaching since the early '70s, and recently taught a Teaching Through Journals course for graduate education students. Susan's e-mail address is s-gardne@wcslc.edu

Joel Greenstein is an Associate Professor of Industrial Engineering at Clemson University although his Ph.D. was in mechanical engineering from the University of Illinois at Urbana-Champaign. His research and teaching interests include human-centered design, human-computer interaction, product and system design and development, and human factors engineering and ergonomics. Some of his educational research is funded by the NSF/SUCCEED Coalition and the NASA Multidisciplinary Design and

Optimization Program to integrate cross-disciplinary education in user-centered design into the engineering curriculum. Joel's e-mail is joel.greenstein@ces.clemson.edu

Michelle Heward is an Assistant Professor of Criminal Justice at Weber State University in Ogden, Utah. After obtaining her J.D. degree from the University of Utah in 1987, she worked in private practice doing civil work, and then as deputy county attorney for Weber County. Her professional interests include juvenile law, civil liability for officers, criminal and constitutional law. In addition to teaching, Michelle is currently setting up youth courts in her area to act as a diversion for minor juvenile offenses. Michelle's e-mail address is mheward@weber.edu

Kelly De Hill is currently General Counsel and Special Assistant to the President at Westminster College in Salt Lake City, Utah, where she was also the Director of the Legal Assistant Certificate Program from 1993–1997. She received her J.D. from the University of Utah where she served as an instructor in the high school with the Utah Law-Related Education Project. Prior to law school, she taught writing and literature in both high school and middle school. Kelly's e-mail address is k-dehill@wcslc.edu

Douglas Hirt is Associate Professor of Chemical Engineering at Clemson University. He received his Ph.D. from Princeton. Doug has been involved with Clemson's Writing-Across-the-Curriculum Program since 1990 and has collaborated with Art Young on journal writing workshops for science and engineering faculty. He received the Dow Outstanding New Faculty Award from the Southeast Section of ASEE in 1995, and he has been involved with SUCCEED, an NSF Engineering Education Coalition, since 1992. Doug's e-mail address is hirtd@clemson.edu

Brian Huot is Associate Professor in the English department at the University of Louisville where he directs the Composition Program. His research interests are primarily in reforming writing assessment practices in and outside the classroom in order to connect assessment to the teaching of writing. He is co-founder and co-editor of *Assessing Writing,* the only journal devoted to writing assessment. He is also a member of the Board of Directors of the Prospect Institute which has advocated alternative assessment and education practices for more than two decades. Brian's e-mail address is bahuot01@homer.louisville.edu

Bobbie Othmer is a Professor of Computer Science at Westminster College of Salt Lake City where she has taught for twelve years. At various times during that period she has been chair of the Computer Science Program and Academic Computing Coordinator. Although she has degrees in math, her doctorate is in Computer Science from Rutgers University. For a few years before coming to Westminster, she was a technical writer and systems programmer. Bobbie's e-mail address is b-othmer@wcslc.edu

Gian Pagnucci, Assistant Professor of English at Indiana University of Pennsylvania, teaches courses on technical writing, electronic literacy, and writing pedagogy in the Rhetoric and Linguistics Graduate Studies Program. Gian has published articles in *English Journal, Theory into Practice, Works and Days,* and *Computers and Composition* as well as NCTE's *The Astonishing Curriculum.* His doctorate is from the University of Wisconsin, and his current research focuses on questions of identity and ethics when teaching in cyberspace and electronic collaboration. Before going into education, Gian spent five years writing computer manuals as a technical writer. Gian's e-mail address is pagnucci@grove.iup.edu

Gail Poirrier is Associate Professor of Nursing at the University of Southwestern Louisiana where she serves as the Acting Dean of the College of Nursing. She is the editor of *Writing-to-Learn: Curricular Strategies for Nursing and Other Disciplines* published in 1996 by the National League for Nursing Press. She serves as a member of the University Writing Advisory Board at USL and is a frequent presenter on Writing Across the Curriculum at such national meetings as the Conference on College Composition and Communication and the biennial WAC conference held in Charleston, SC. Gail's e-mail address is jdc6124@usl.edu

Alan Rogers is Professor of Accounting at Westminster College of Salt Lake City with an MBA from the University of Utah. He has been at Westminster for nineteen years and is an award-winning teacher. Alan is also a CPA, and he keeps current in the field by doing sabbaticals at such prestigious accounting firms as Coopers and Lybrand. Every December Alan runs a tax institute for local CPAs, and he has his own private accounting practice involving consulting, auditing, and taxes.

Terry Scott is Associate Professor of Computer Science at University of Northern Colorado in Greeley, where he has taught for the last thirteen years. Although his B.S. (Iowa State University) and Ph.D. (University of Wyoming) degrees are in physics, Terry received an M.S. in Computer Science from Kansas State University. His interests in computer science are computer architecture/organization, digital logic, computer graphics, the teaching of computer science, and developing software to help in the teaching of computer science. Terry's e-mail address is tscott@fisher.UnivNorthCo.EDU

Jerry VanOs is Professor of Accounting/Management Information Systems (MIS) at Westminster College of Salt Lake City. He has been at Westminster ten years and served as the MBA Program Director for the last eight. Jerry's Ph.D. is from Brigham Young University, and he also holds CPA and CMA certifications. Jerry teaches a variety of courses dealing with systems–accounting information systems, management information systems, and systems analysis and design. Before becoming a faculty member, Jerry worked in both public and private accounting, the latter for a Fortune 500 company. Currently he has been traveling the country as part of the CPA Vision Project, which is designed to help accountants redefine their mission for the year 2000 and beyond. Jerry's e-mail is j-vanos@wcslc.edu

Keith Vogt is President of the Telis Foundation, a nonprofit educational organization dedicated to infusing technology resources into schools, particularly Internet access. Telis also develops and makes available online educational resources for teachers and parents. A former elementary school principal, classroom teacher, and small business owner, he recently served as Director of the Department of Education's California Technology Project. He is an adjunct instructor in the College of Education, California State University, Long Beach. Keith's e-mail address is kvogt@telis.org

MaryEllen Vogt is Associate Professor of Education at California State University, Long Beach. A former classroom teacher and reading specialist, she received her doctorate in Language and Literacy from the University of California, Berkeley. She co-authored *Portfolios in Teacher Education, Professional Portfolio Models: Applications in Education,* and *What a Difference a Phoneme Makes! A Teacher's Guide to the English Language.* She has served as President of the California Reading Association and member of the Executive Board of the International Reading Association. She has made professional presentations on reading for school districts and professional associations throughout the United States and in Canada, Argentina, Estonia, and Hungary. Currently, she is involved in the "Reading and Writing for Critical Thinking" project co-sponsored by the International Reading Association. MaryEllen's e-mail address is mvogt@telis.org

Kathleen Blake Yancey is Associate Professor of English at the University of North Carolina Charlotte where she teaches courses in first-year writing, methods of teaching, rhetorical theory, and writing assessment. A former middle school teacher, she has worked with faculty across the country on projects including classroom assessment, Writing Across the Curriculum, program assessment, and reflective teaching. Her most recent publications include the co-edited volume *Assessing Writing Across the Curriculum* and the monograph *Reflection in the Writing Classroom.* With Brian Huot, she founded and edits the journal *Assessing Writing.* Kathleen's e-mail address is kbyancey@newmail.uncc.edu